FAITH *in a* FOXHOLE

War Letters to Home

MARVIN WILLIAM GOLDER
with JOHN F. WALSH ·

Compiled by Beth Miglio

Aperture Press

To the memory of Nana and Pop Pop

Janet Mitchell Golder (1922–2003)
Marvin William Golder (1918–2006)

Contents

—

Foreword

—

Some moments in your life stay with you forever. I remember this one as if it happened yesterday. I was about 14 and sitting in Nana and Pop Pop's kitchen in their house on Orange Street. I was asking Nana questions about World War II. Nana never went into great detail about the war, all she would say to me is "we did what we had to do" and "I prayed your grandfather would return safely". She kept her faith and waited for the letters from Pop Pop. I asked her "Where are the letters?" She said they had saved a few letters, but they didn't want them read until they both passed away. Of course, I wanted to see them and was concerned they would never be located. Nana assured me she kept them in a place they would be found. I promised her I wouldn't read them until they both passed away; I kept that promise.

I found the letters in the bottom drawer of Nana's dresser while Pop Pop was very sick. We read the first one together, as a family a few days after Pop Pop died. I realized the letters contained a great deal of history and my grandparent's life. I felt strongly they not only needed to be preserved, but shared with the family and future generations. I believe we can all learn from the sacrifices, faith and courage they both had during a very difficult and uncertain time in their lives. We can never forget what they did for our country and how brave and courageous they were during this time. Many people and countries were liberated and given back their freedoms, because of their sacrifices.

Now, I have often wondered if Nana knew these letters would have more meaning after their passing. It was her way of reminding us to cherish what was essential to them: faith in God, family, service to your country, and community.

I have found a great deal of comfort in Pop Pop's words he left behind for us; it's as if he is speaking to me today. I know if he had faith inside a foxhole, it is possible for all of us to hold onto our faith outside of one.

Introduction

—

On October 30, 1941 Marvin William Golder married Janet Mitchell. It was Bill's 23rd birthday and Janet was 19 years old. They could not have known that by the year's end their country would enter a world war. The war would impact both of them and their faith.

Years prior to passing, my grandparents sat down in their home on Orange Street in Berwick, Pennsylvania; and reread the entire letter collection. Together they decided which letters would be kept for the family and which ones would be destroyed.

What remains are twenty six letters written by Bill Golder to Janet Golder, my grandparents. The first letter from the collection was written on April 19, 1945, 9 ½ months after Bill entered the war in Europe.

I will never be certain why these are the letters they chose to save; perhaps these share the most details of what the war was like for my grandfather. The end of the war was in sight and "Victory in Europe" VE day was to come on May 9th, 1945. Until this time details of the war went unwritten in his correspondence back home. He didn't want to worry his wife; and she had much to worry about.

Bill's journey into war started years earlier. On August 23, 1943 he entered the United States Army. After completing basic training he was stationed at Camp Rucker,

Alabama with the 35th Infantry Division, 320th Infantry Regiment, Cannon Company.

In mid November, his unit traveled to Nashville, Tennessee to partake in training maneuvers. It was during this time that Janet traveled to Tennessee to see her husband. I recall her telling me the story many times. She had to drive alone to Tennessee. However, with the gasoline rations, there would not be enough gas to make a return trip. Her father, Harry Mitchell came up with the extra gas and hid several cans in the trunk of her car. She never found out how he came up with the additional gas, but she was worried the entire trip that she would be caught. Small price to pay, knowing this might be the last opportunity to see Bill before he went off to war. In the weeks that followed Janet found out what a blessing the trip was, she was expecting their first child.

After completing training in Tennessee Bill's unit was sent to Camp Butner, NC and was prepared for shipment overseas. They would be stationed in NC until early May 1944; then they traveled to Camp Kilmer, NJ for overseas preparation. On May 12, Bill boarded the Edmund B. Alexander in New York and set off for a two week voyage to Liverpool England. While in England his unit attended classes and trained for their entry into war.

On July 6th (D-Day plus 30) after making the voyage across the English Channel Bill's regiment landed on Omaha Beach near Isigny, Normandy. He had entered the war in Europe.

At this time, Janet was now 7 months pregnant with their first child. She was living with her father Harry Mitchell in her childhood home. War was not unfamiliar to Harry, a veteran of World War I. He was a tough, loud man with a tender heart. His large stature was fitting with his personality. Harry was a generous man who was known to pull money from his wallet if someone was in need. When he wasn't involved in republican politics, he could be found hunting with his dogs or fishing the local Pennsylvania rivers or streams.

Janet's mother Margaret Mitchell died at age 44, from complications from surgery. Her death came one day before Janet's 21st birthday on February 8, 1943— the same year Bill was drafted into the Army. Margaret was known as a kind and loving women who always got pleasure in cooking for others, something Janet would carry on in her life. The large attendance at Margaret's funeral was a testament to how much she had meant to people. Many people had traveled a great distance to attend, which wasn't as easy as it would be today.

Bill and Janet's baby girl, Kathleen Margaret Golder, was born on September 3rd, 1944. On that day Bill's unit was Joinville France.

Weeks later, Bill was being shelled upon and his only protection was an uncovered foxhole. He turned to his faith and said the Lord's Prayer. I can never know for sure, but I wonder if my great grandfather shared the same experience during the Great War. Harry knelt next to his bed every night, opened a prayer book, and prayed aloud.

In the months ahead Bill's unit would help to liberate Normandy, France, Belgium, Luxembourg, Holland, and Germany. They earned five battle Campaign Stars.

During this entire time period Janet was home with her newborn baby. She didn't know if or when she would see her husband again. She struggled with the limited resources that were available during this time. Most of what we consider basic needs such as gas, sugar, and coffee were being rationed. She made it through this difficult time by putting her faith and trust in God. These same beliefs are stated in every letter my grandfather wrote.

I transcribed the letters just as they were written, and made no corrections to spelling or grammar. It was important to me to preserve them in actual form. I have gotten a great deal of inspiration and sense of who my grandparents were by reading these letters. I hope by preserving this history the future generations will know what life was like during the war and why they are called the "greatest generation".

Soldier Answers His Girl

by Sergeant John Rice

Dear sweetheart, you're so far away
I need you so my dear,
I feel the same as you.
I'm longing for you here.

Strange patterns have the stars giv'n out;
It makes our lives as one
I know that since we've met
Our life has just begun.

There is no one else but you
And I feel the same strain,
It makes me very glad
And somehow like a pain.

Since the days of Ancient Egypt
It never could be stilled,
`Til I have you in my arms
And all our love fulfilled.

*This poem was in my grandfather's WWII
photo collection.*

Part One

—

LETTERS HOME

by PFC Marvin W. Golder
April–September 1945

Marvin William Golder
"Pop Pop"

19 April 1945
Somewhere in Germany

My Dearest Darling Janet and Kathy,

Last night, darling, I hit the jack pot. I received 5 letters from you, one from Jane, one from Carl May. One from mother, the G.I. Extra and an Enterprise.

I am going to do my best and ans. All the questions I can now. I don't know how much time I will have but here goes.

I am sorry to hear bout Chas Hill I hope he wasn't wounded too bad.

Kathy really must be some girl, I can hardly wait to see her. You tell me everything about her so I feel as if I really know my daughter quite well. Strange isn't it?

I am glad Joy has a boy now, I guess that is what they wanted. If you see her tell her I ask about them all.

Darling I know how you feel on holidays, I feel the same way but I guess we will just have to bear it—for a while. You have been a very brave girl these past 20 ms. And I admire you so very much for it. I have a lot to thank you for. I really mean that kitten.

You sure did have a big dinner, boy I sure would have given anything to have been there. That menu, boy what a feed. Our home has'nt changed any and I am sure glad of that. Ha!

I know Kathy takes after you now when you say she

adores family dinners, God bless her. I pray to God that I will be able to eat thanksgiving dinner in my own home. We must trust in the Lord to make it possible.

I am very glad mother gave you those nice gifts. In her letter she told me she was down and Kathy went to sleep in her arms. In every letter I get from her she raves about Kathy.

Darling I don't want you to think that half of the trouble is your fault because it is'nt. I know better than that. You a scatter-brain? Far from it. Don't ever think that of yourself. There is nothing wrong with you at all. You are doing a wonderful job of being a mother and a wife. No one can tell me any different. You are very very efficient—the best.

I am afraid I won't be very firm with Kathy. You know me, I am too soft. I guess something will have to be done to show her who is boss. We both will have to be firm!

You really had a big day Easter, it is a wonder you stayed up that long. I don't blame you for not writing, after all you had a very hard day.

I bet that was a swell orchid I know how you always like them. Your dad sure is helping me out in many things. He is giving you some of the things I can't. He certainly is a swell father-in-law. No better one around.

I guess Jane is receiving some competion in letter writing, You my dear are doing fine, I do enjoy your letters so very much I know it is impossible to write long ones every day. I enjoy each and every one of your letters. They make the going a hell of a lot smoother.

Is this house Annabell and Joe moving into as nice as the one on Market St? That sure seems like a lot of rent and have to heat it too. I guess houses are very scarce and you must take the first one you can get. I am very very sorry to hear Ann lost the baby. I know how much they want a family and how they were counting on it. I suppose they both feel very bad. There must be something very wrong, I hope she can get straightened out.

I guess there is'nt much I can say about you working so hard, I do wish you would take it a little easy. I know you are a very hard worker and that you have more work that Kathy is here but try darling not to over do it. That is all I will say—But Listen!

I wish I would have stayed in Holland longer, I know my little Dutch girl friend would have loved to have a doll from the states. I don't suppose I'll ever get back to Belfeld, but you never can tell I might—after the war. I am glad you liked her picture. She sure is sweet. She did remind me that I have a daughter of my own. I guess that is why I took to her so good. I seem to be her favorite American during my stay there. Of course I did bribe her by giving here candy bars and chewing gum. (which she would chew 2 to 3 sticks at a time) She was some kid.

It is funny that Kathy knows when you go out, she sure is a mothers girl, I do hope you can break her of that.

I suppose when I come home she will call me "Grandpa" what I am saying, I hope I don't look that old.

Oh yes the Pacific question—well we don't know what will happen naturally we don't want to go, I think 9 mos and maybe more of combat is enough for any man. I see in the S&S that all ablebodied men who have'nt been overseas will be sent over and vets will take their places—that's for me. I'm not worrying about the Pacific because it won't do a bit of good. If the Army says Pacific, I guess I'll go. I love my country enough to do that. I would much rather come home, which I hope it turns out that way. I'd much rather be in the Army of occupation than go to the Pacific. Well time will tell everything and we must put our trust in God. That is what I am doing. If that is his will, it shall be done.

I hope Kathy is much better now, I suppose that cold and cutting teeth has made her very sick. Now that she is cutting teeth you might have her sick more often. I hope not because I know how much that worries you. I am glad to hear that she was better. I hate to have her sick, she really has been a good baby.

I don't know what was the matter with me when I said I wish we had a brass knocker, after I read your letter It reminded me you telling me you had chimes. Boy me and my one track mind. I'd rather have the chimes any day.

I really hated to say anything about the cigarettes

you are sending me. I know you are doing your very best. Camels and Luckies will be swell. Forgive me again darling.

That Dr. of ours is one swell fellow, If I can find something over here that I think he might like I am going to send it to him. He has been wonderful to us and has kept my mind at ease so much in knowing he is taking care of you and Kathy so well.

Thanks darling for the $5.00, I'll sure be able to use it. I sure have been cut short but it was worth it.

Tell Nina that husband of her's is crazy. I really enjoyed his letter very much. He said you two devils are spoiling Kathy. He said when she gets older it will be daddy get me this get me that. He says see what the devils are doing to shorty. What a guy. I must write to him very soon.

Mother sent me some stamps, I guess because the last letter I wrote to her I sent it free. She said it took five weeks. I believe she has a swell job now, she seems to think it will be ok. It sounds good to me. I do hope she gets something easy at her age she should.

Jane wrote to me from the Lutheran Church Center for service men. Midge belongs to the Lutheran Church and she (Midge) was working as hostess and Jane went along for something to do. The way Jane described the place it is quite nice. I sure wish I were at some servicemen center in the U.S.A.

Oh, yes last night I also got the power of attorney now as soon as I get it filled out and signed I'll send it to you. It may be a little while because we are moving so fast that it is hard to get anything done. I must go to reg to have it witnessed. I'll do it as soon as I can because I know you want it.

Darling another thing I've been going to tell you and that is it at anytime you must get in touch with me for any reason, go to the Red Cross, things there move very fast. Say that someone gets very sick and the Dr though I should be home, if he goes to the Red Cross and request my presents nine times out of ten I'd be there. The Red Cross will be able to do wonders. I thought I'd better tell you so that if you ever needed to get word to me for any reason that is the way to go about it. Of course that example I gave above is not as simple as all that I guess they have to check and all that. I suppose Dr S. knows all about that. I though I'd better tell you about it because I've seen it work over here and it is ok.

Yesterday we got PX and cigarette rations In our PX rations we got two cokes, 3 bars of candy, two cigars, two pks of chewing gum. In our cig rations we got two pks of cigarettes, and two candy bars, cig are getting kind of short these days.

Its kind of cool to-day although the sun is shinning. We have been having some very nice days. I hope it stays nice for many months to come.

I heard last night that the Russians has started a drive, I sure hope that is so because we will soon be meeting them. The sooner we meet the sooner this war will be over.

I wrote to mother yesterday so now I'll have to write to here again to-day.

I have a little time this morning so I am going to try and get caught up on my letter writing. I know my letters to you have been very very short and I sure hate to write I saw a good dog-fight this morning. Four of our P-51's knocked down 3 German planes. Boy here on the front we see everything first hand—which sometimes to fast!

Art got a box from his girl last night. He got two bottles of coke and some marshmallows and candy.

Darling those five letters I got from you last night were so swell. I enjoyed every word of them. You do write such good ones. Gosh darling I do love and adore you so very much. I miss you more and more each day. I just hope it won't be many more months till we will be together.

Art and I have been talking about the war—we don't hear any news at all in fact the radio isn't even giving any out. There is an Anti Aircraft unit next to us and we listened to the news last night but they did'nt say much. In fact most of the fronts are blacked out. I sure wish we'd hear something. I am anxious to hear how things are going.

Well darling I guess this is about all I have for my

report from Germany for to-day.

My dearest Janet I do love and adore you with all my heart, soul, and body. God bless you and Kathy and may he keep you both safe from all harm.

My most sincere and deepest love and million kisses.

Your husband,
Bill

April 19, 1945: Photos

~

Janet and Kathy, 1944

April 22, 1945
Somewhere in Germany

My Dearest Darling Janet and Kathy,

Good morning my dearest. It is a cloudy Sunday morning. The sun was out for a while this morning but it has gone in again.

We have church at 1:30 this afternoon. I want to go. I hope I have time. I say that because I am going to Regt to get those papers signed for you. I have to go right after dinner so I hope I can get it done after dinner so I hope I can get it done before 1:30. They told us this morning that church was at 9:45 so Art and I went but no church til 1:30.

This morning I got another picture of myself. It was taken in Gremacy Forest (France) last Oct. As you can see I am quite dirty and was in the process of washing up. You can also see my combat inf badge. My hair is still a bit short from having it almost all off in July. I hope you like this one if you don't I am sure it would scare the rats away if you put it in the cellar.

We got cigarette rations to-day. We got 7 pks of cigarettes—now that is more like it. I was completely out.

We did have mail call yesterday (last night) but I did not receive any at all.

I should write to Paul this afternoon, I have time now. I don't think I am behind any of my letters, for a change.

I am going to keep this letter going for a while to-day maybe I can work a good long one out of it. Being to-day is our day I like to write as much as I can.

I had another dream about you the other night, I remember we had gone to bed and we curled up like we always did, boy I hated to wake up—because that is as far as it went—dam it! I couldn't even stay and finish the night out. That is the trouble with dreams, they end at the wrong time and place.

Well, darling I think I stop for a while I'll write more this afternoon—see you then.

Here I am again. I just came back from church. The Chaplin had a very good sermon. I enjoyed it very much. The church was a very old one. It is a bit smaller then ours (Episcopal). We will have church in regular church now. I am glad of it. We have since we've been in combat been in barns, schools bombed and shelled building and even out side, so a church is a really added comfort.

I also got the power of attorney signed and I am sending it in an other envelop. There are 5 copies and I have the original. I don't think you'll need that. I could send it too, I may yet.

It is a real April day-showers every once in a while. Right now, the sun is out but before long I suppose it will be raining.

I miss you very much to-day Janet dear. I guess Sunday, church and walking alone though this German town back from church makes those little things we did really come back. I hope before long that I'll be back with you on our Sundays and that we will be able to do those things we once did.

I can't help but feel that this war won't last much longer. Things are getting very tight for the Germans. It will be like they say there won't really be a certain V-E Day but a gradual cease firing here and there. That is in process in many places at this moment. The Ruhr pocket is an example of what I mean. I guess we will have to pocket them and then widdle them down from there. I see in the S&S that there is no more Western Front. Lets pray this cutting off and reducing system soon pays off and that there won't be any more German Army to cause us any trouble.

I just heard the news on the radio and it really sounds wonderful. Another month will really tell a great story. Who knows maybe it won't be that long.

We have 10 in 1 today and they are a new type. They had caned hamburgers, caned fruit cocktail and caned fruit cake. I was unlucky and did not get the Hamburg but I got the fruit cocktail. We were all surprised to see that kind of rations. I don't know if they changed supper or not, I'll learn when we go to chow to-night. I'll finish this letter to-night. I want to wait for mail call before I close. I may get some mail. I believer I'll stop for now but will be back later.

I just received a letter from you (April 11) and a letter from Geo C. Geo was wounded March 4. He said he did not tell Ann how bad he was hurt but he said it really wasn't too bad. I must write to him to-night. He is in England, he also sent regards to you.

So you did not like my German paper? Well I don't blame you, it took too dam much ink anyway.

I am really behind times when I said Kathy would be 17 mo old next Easter. I guess I can't add (still!)

Yes, Art received Kathy's Easter card, I am afraid he won't write and thank you because he is not a writing man. He has a hard time writing to his parents and his girl. He said thanks for everything.

I am very glad to hear Kathy is much better, that makes me feel better. I guess the fresh air and sunshine really does her a world of good.

We are told we are going to hear some very good news to-night, I don't know what it is. Maybe if I do find out I won't be able to write about it. I have a very good idea what it is. That is all I will say now. I hope I'll be able to break something good. We shall see.

I forget I had my picture taken again, The First Sgt took it this afternoon. I'll have more pictures when the fellows get them back.

Boy it is really raining again. About 5 min ago the sun was out—Fine weather! The boys want me to play pinochle again to-night, so I guess I will.

Well darling I guess this is all I have for my report from Germany. If anything that I can tell comes around I'll add it later.

My dearest darling I do love and adore you with all my heart, soul and body. God bless you and Kathy and may he keep you both safe and sound from all harm.

My sincere and deepest love and a million kisses.

Your husband,
Bill

April 23, 1945
Somewhere in Germany

My Dearest Darling Janet and Kathy,

Well darling what they told us last night, was very good news. As yet I can't tell you what it is but you won't have to worry about me anymore. At least for a long long time. I do wish I could tell you the whole story but not as yet. I can assure you it is the best deal we've had since we've been in the E.T.O I suppose later I can tell you everything.

It is now 2:45, I will not finish this letter until after mail call.

We have been having April showers again. It is rather cool too.

The war news gets better by the hr. I really haven't heard any to-day but last night things were very very good. We expect any day for Gen Ike to say all organized resistance has ceased maybe by the time you receive this letter it will be over.

We had a very good dinner this noon, we had liver, onions, mashed potatoes, gravy, peas, pineapple, bread and coffee. I know I don't usually eat liver but that was the first I've had any for over a year and it tasted very good.

As yet I have'nt written to Geo and Paul. I must do it to-night. We played pinackle til late last night, we played all morning and we play all afternoon till just now.

Tomorrow we are going to take showers. I'll be glad of that, I am really dirty my hair is so full of sand it is'nt even funny. I won't have to worry about sand any more.

Say, how about some half and half? I am out again and lately we have'nt been getting much tobacco. If you can send me some. If you can't get half and half get anything but Duco! Tell dad I don't like his favorite tobacco.

I suppose he has smoked most of my pipes—with Duco! Remember...

The rest of this letter is missing.

Written on the back of the envelope is a note:

"Love to the best mother in the world.
Both Well—God Bless you.
Paul"

April 24, 1945
Somewhere in Germany

My Dearest Darling Janet and Kathy,

Good afternoon my darling. How is my wonderful wife to-day?

Last night I went to the movies right after I finished writing to you. I saw "Hollywood Canteen" it was very good. I don't know if we are going to have any movies or not to-night. I hope we do. I still have'nt fixed my bed like I want to, so I guess I'll have to wait till to-morrow.

I am on K.P. to-day. We had to have one man out of our section so I said I'd take it first. It is 2:15 and I've done all my after dinner work. So I won't have much to do till supper time.

I haven't heard any war news for about two days so I don't know how things are going.

So far to-day I have'nt much new, I am going to finish this letter to-night when the mail comes in.

It has been a nice day, except a bit cool. How is the weather at home? Is it warm?

I am writing this letter in the mess hall, a very nice place to.

As yet I haven't written to Geo or Paul I must do that as soon as I get a chance.

We got cigarette rations to-day. I got 7 pks (I believe

I just glanced at them) of cigarettes, candy, chewing gum, half and half, shaving cream, soap, matches.

Well darling I believe I stop for now. I write more as soon as we have mail call. See you then.

Back again darling, I just finished K.P I did not receive any mail to-day in fact there were only packages. Well to-morrow is another day.

I must clean my rifle to-night we are having grd inspection. I won't have time to write to Geo and Paul to-night. I must clean the rifle.

I'll have some pictures of one of the worse crimes the Germans committed to date. Janet you can't believe what those German's have done. Those pictures are very hard to look at but they show what the Germans are and what they have done. I wish everyone in the U.S. could see it. This is not just some allied propaganda it is true I've seen it with my own eyes. It is a sight that will stay with you as long as you live.

I don't have any news of importance to-day. This looks like it will be short letter. I shouldn't write short one now because I'll have plenty of time to write.

I hope I can soon tell you what someday I know it will please you very very much. I know I like it.

Last night in that picture "Hollywood Canteen" I heard for the first time "Don't fence me in" it is a swell tune. I guess I am a little behind times but I finally heard it.

I think if I find out where Foster is I maybe able to go

and see him we are in a position now where I believe we may go and visit our friends. I am really not sure about that. I must find out more.

Well darling this is about all I have for my report from Germany. Oh yes, Art said he would write to you and that was a promise.

My dearest I do love and adore you with all my heart soul and body. God bless you and Kathy and may he keep you both safe from all harm.

My most sincere and deepest love and million kisses.

Your husband,
Bill

April 24, 1945: Photos and Facts

~

The atrocities that were mentioned in this letter took place at Gardelegen, Germany. Bill had several photos that were taken at this location. On the back of these photos, he wrote about the brutality at Gardelegen and what he had witnessed.

Bill wrote on the back of the photo: "Here is where the dirty work was done. At this door one Russian tried to get out, he got his head and shoulder out but that was all. Maybe you saw the picture in Life Mag. If you did-that was it. I was there when Life photograph that picture. In my letter I am not sure I spelled the name of the camp

right most of us forgot the name but not the sight.

"Here we see more civilians digging. "I don't think this needs any explaining-does it?" That clothing belonged-once-to the victims."

Written on the back of this photo: "Here the civilians are waiting to be told where they are to dig the graves. Note the sheets under their arms. They put the victims in the sheets and then they were buried. The building in the background is where the Russians were burned. The white tape is to mark off the graves."

Bill wrote on the back of the photo: "Here German civilians are digging the graves-note the expression on the faces of the Germans. They are not a happy lot. Behind them sits a Sherman tank, machine gun fully loaded-it was used twice. The civilians were men from all walks of life, Drs, store keepers, farmers, ect. Each dug graves and picked that dirty rotten, burnt, smelly flesh up and layed it in a sheet and buried it.

"I think this picture speaks for its self. I only have half of the graves on this picture! Well I guess not even half."

April 25, 1945
Somewhere in Germany

My Dearest Darling Janet and Kathy,

Good morning my dearest. It is a beautiful morning. There is'nt a cloud in the sky and it is'nt so cold.

I'll probably keep this letter going all day, I don't know if we will do anything or not today.

I wrote a letter to Jane last night, then we played cards til 11:00.

I don't have much news this morning, it seems lately I don't say much of anything.

One of the fellows got some funny books so I can spend a little time this morning reading. We had fried eggs this morning, I sure enjoy fried eggs. I'd like to have some fried eggs and ham for a change. That would really be good.

I finally took my bed roll apart and got it cleaned. I had more dam sand in that roll. It was really dirty.

Darling I believe I'll stop for a while, I'll be back later.

It is now 3:30 we just had mail call, I did not get any mail from you to-day. I did get letters from Jane, mother and Emily.

Jane wrote me a short letter, mother was telling me about her Kingston job.

Emily was telling me about Martha, I guess she broke

her engagement to that fellow.

Jane see Bob S was wounded, I feel sorry for him. I saw where the wound he got will leave him with a scare. He was good looking kid, I sure hope it does'nt maim his looks any.

I also received two Enterprises to-day. I see the old town is the same. I do hope before long that I'll be back in that best city in the world.

We got some mag. This afternoon, one Life, Newsweek, Readers Digest, Aero Digest and one funny book.

Darling I am going to soon stop because I want to mail this letter when I go to supper.

I don't know if we will have any movies or not to-night. I have'nt heard anything about it. I sure hope we do.

The Germans say they heard over the radio that the war is over. They all seemed very happy—I don't know if there is anything to it or not. I sure hope so.

Well darling I guess this is all I have for my report from Germany to-day.

My dearest darling I do love and adore you with all my heart, soul and body.

God bless you and Kathy and may he keep you both safe and sound from all harm. My most sincere and deepest love and a million kisses.

Your husband,
Bill

April 27, 1945
Somewhere in Germany

My Dearest Darling Janet and Kathy:

It is now about 11:15 and we will soon eat dinner. I know it must be almost time because I am very hungry.

We are going to have showers this afternoon, I may take one, I did have a bath before yesterday.

I expect to go fishing in a canal before many days. We are trying to get fishing equipment now. You can see what I mean where I said we have the best deal we ever had. I hope it keeps up for quite sometime. It looks like it will too.

I just finished dinner. We had hamburgers, mashed potatoes, gravy, peas, beans, peaches, bread, Jam and coffee. It was a very good meal.

I go on guard to-night, I don't know what time I go on. We form at 7:45 I hope I get some mail before that. Last night I went to bed early and the mail came in about 9:45, I got two Enterprise that is all I got. I hope I get some to-day.

It has been cloudy all day, in fact a while this morning it rained but it has stopped now.

I really have'nt much news to-day, as usual I'll keep this letter going all day in hopes that I get some mail. To-day would be a swell day to write all those back letters I owe, I may get some ambitious and write this afternoon. It seems the more time I have the less I write. I guess I'd better get on the ball.

I am going to leave you for a while, I'll be back later.

Here I am again, it's 5:45 I just finished supper.

I layed down at about 2:00 and slept til 4:45. You see what I mean when I say I have a lot of time to write but don't do it.

I really have been relaxing this last week. After 9 ½ months war I feel in need of a lot of rest.

I think I've seen by last day of combat here in Europe. I pray to God that I won't have any more to go through—here or in the Pacific. If I have to go to the Pacific-well, I'll just have too. I know I can come through that on as well as the European war. I have that much faith in God.

As far as this point system goes, I only hope I have enough points to keep me from going to the Pacific. I'd rather get Army of Occupation any time. Well I don't think it will be many more weeks til we find out what is what.

I am afraid I won't be able to wait for mail call to finish this letter. I go on guard at 7:45 and I don't believe the mail will come in before that. If I get any mail I can ans it to-morrow. Then maybe I'll be able to write a long letter. I would have a lot to tell if I could but for the present no sale!

It won't be long till the first of May, it will be so good

to have summer here. After going through a rough winter, I am more than glad to see a good weather come.

Well darling I believe this is about all I have for my report from Germany to-day.

My dearest I do love and adore you with all my heart, soul and body. God bless you and Kathy and may he keep you both safe from all harm.

My most sincere and deepest love and a million kisses.

Your Husband,
Bill

April 29, 1945

8:15 PM Sunday
Somewhere in Germany

My Dearest Darling Janet and Kathy:

No one got any mail to-night, so I decided to start a letter to you to-night.

We had church at 1:00 this afternoon but I did not go. I stay in all afternoon and slept. I did read a while then I went to sleep. I guess I should have went but I was kinda tired.

It had been very cold to-day and a fire feels dam good.

I did not get guard to-day I suppose I'll get it to-morrow night, either that or K.P. I don't care, I am having a swell time just resting, reading and taking it easy.

I am reading a very good mystery it is entitled "Blood upon the Snow" I got started this afternoon and am about half way through it now. I suppose I'll get through it by to-morrow.

I am still behind in my writing, I don't what the matter is with me but I just don't have any ambition to write too any one but you. I usually ans those letters as soon as I get them but now that I have the time I just can't seem to get it done. I am going to try and work on a few to-morrow.

I think I'll go to bed early to-night I want to read a little longer then I'll turn in.

Daring I am very lonesome, you know how I feel. I am alone in my room now and I sure do miss you. Sunday nights bring back a lot of memories, don't they? I do wish I had you on my lap now and that we were listening to the radio. When I write and tell you how I miss you I always fee better afterwards, I guess I write what my heart feels. I don't like to say I feel lonesome because it makes you feel bad and Lord knows I want my letters to cheer you up. I feel better already just telling you all this. We both miss each other very much and we know it very well. Gosh Jan darling I hope we soon will be to-gether, this being with out you so long is really tough. I long to see Kathy too and to let her know her father, I do hope she likes her dad. I suppose you have told her everything nice about me (and stink!!) I guess she will find out the bad in me soon enough with out you telling here! I think a lot of my (our) daughter and I can say she is in for a lot of spoiling, because everyone has had a head start on me. I'll have my fun when I come home. I suppose now she is quite spoiled—the little dear.

I am afraid I won't be very firm with her as soon as she turns a sad eye on me I am finished, she'll get anything I can possible buy her there are two girls in this world I am madly in love with, they are two of the most wonderful girls in this earth. My whole aim in life is to keep them free from want-always-and to have everything money can buy. I do hope I can achieve that goal.

Well Kitten we got our rations to-day. I got 7 pks of cig, five candy bars, shaving cream, soap and matches. I gave away 6 candy bars for two pks of cig. I don't care much for that candy and I had 13 bars any way. So now I have 13 pks of cig. I had 5 left from last week, I really surprised myself. I am cutting down.

Darling I believe I will stop for to-night. May God watch over you and protect yu through this night my love. A good night kiss and my very deepest love darling. I'll see you in the morning. Your Bill

April 30, 1945 (letter continued)
8:30 AM

Good morning my darling. Another cold day to-day. It is partly cloudy this morning. It rained quite hard last night but so far to-day we have no rain.

We are getting our duffel bags to-day, I don't have much in mine, so it won't take long to clean it out.

I don't know if I will have guard or not to-night, I look for it, either guard or K.P. I'll be very surprised if I don't get one of them.

Again I don't have very much news, that line is getting old is'nt it? I guess it is the best I can think of.

I read a while after I finished my letter to you last night. I got so sleepy I was reading one page a couple of times, so I thought that was time to stop.

I washed and shaved this morning after breakfast that sure made me feel better.

To-day I am going to try and write some more letters, I must get them written. I wrote more letters when I did'nt have the time that I do now.

If it ever get really nice I am going to borrow Someones camera and take some pictures of these windmills around here. I also want to take pictures of the country side. I believe you will enjoy them—if I take them. I hope I can borrow a camera.

We get payed to-day, I owe only one dollar so with the six that I already have I should have about $25.00. It is nice for a change, to have some money now all I need is a pass—to someplace!

Well Kitten I guess I've just about told you all the news in my report from Germany.

My darling Janet I do love and adore you with all my heart, soul and body. God bless you and Kathy and may he keep you safe from all harm. My most sincere and deepest love and a million kisses.

Your Husband,
Bill

April 30, 1945

Somewhere in Germany

My Dearest Darling Janet and Kathy,

This evening I received you April 22, letter. I also got a letter from Jean and mother.

Darling I do hope that soldier knows what he is talking about. I am praying to God, so I must trust in Him.

I am glad that Aunt Mary got down for the week-end, I understand why you did not write think nothing of it.

So Kathy can say DaDa, I guess I'd better get home so she can see who she is calling DaDa. I am glad you explained to her but I don't think she quite understands—yet.

Well that is a surprise Jeanette having a baby, I never thought they would myself. I am glad for them maybe they will settle down. I hope they do. I always like them dispite their funny ways.

I guess you are having cold weather at home like we are having. Well to-morrow is the 1st of May so maybe in a few weeks warmer weather will come to stay. I don't mind it so much being in a house.

There was'nt too much to ans in your letter but I must say that letter was a swell moral builder. I never saw it to fail when I seem a little blue you are always there with something to cheer me up. That is just one of the many things I love about you, even these many miles you give me hope and courage. Remember when I came home from work a bit depressed how you made things so much better and they always were too. I suppose the day I wrote that letter I was disgusted but I am all over that now. I should know better, things are never as bad as they seem. I seen that many times.

I know I must never loose faith in God, he helped you to bring into this world a wonderful daughter and he has kept me from all harm—and I've really had some close ones. So I know he is helping us in every way.

I am on guard to-night. I go on at 8 and go off at 10:00, then on at 2 to 4. I don't go on again til 2pm to-morrow afternoon. That is'nt a bad shift.

We got or duffle bags this morning. My civilian shoes are still good (I just ran out of ink. I'll have to finish this in pencil) My bed room slippers are ok I am sure going to use them. I also got the cigarette lighter fixed and now that works.

I counted the letters I received from you from May to Oct. I had them all in my bag—there were over 100, about 106 to be exact. I burned all the old ones but yours I am keeping them. I read over quite a few of them, they sure do tell a lot about our lives. How we whistled in the dark about the war being over soon – but now it will soon be a reality.

Janet I put my blouse on to-day and—I can hardly get into it. It was a 36. When I gave my size for the new blouse I said 34—boy I really screw up on that. I did have a sweater on and that may have made a difference but still I know I've gotten a lot stouter. I'll have to do something about getting that size changed.

I really feel swell the best I've felt since I've been overseas.

I still have'nt written to anyone since yesterdays letters-wrong since Sat. I ordered 50 stamps to-day so as soon as I get them I must do some tall writing.

I see I am getting your mail in 8 days now, I think that is swell.

Tell mother I'll write as soon as I get some stamps which should be in a very few days.

I finished that book I was telling you about, it was very good and I enjoyed it very much.

It seems like I had something else to tell you but I can't remember of it now.

Do you remember last Oct I told you I had a paper about the Okehampton Castle? I was going to send it too you but then I could'nt find it. Well to-day I did find it so I'll send it to you later. I'll send it in its own envelope, right now I don't have the stamps. I am going to have to borrow an envelope to send this letter.

It seems to be clearing off now, I sure hope the 1st of May is a real nice day.

I was just looking at your picture again- darling I can't put into words how beautiful you are getting you are really lovely. Gosh Jan dear I do love you so very much. I hope it won't be long till I'll be holding you so very tight in my arms. What sure will be a wonderful day.

It won't be long now till I'll have to go on guard, so I guess I'd better close now. I guess this is all of my report from Germany to-day.

My darling wife I do love and adore you with all my heart, soul and body. God bless you and Kathy and may He keep you safe and sound from all harm. My most sincere and deepest love and a million kisses.

Your Husband,
Bill

May 1, 1945
Somewhere in Germany

My Dearest Darling Janet and Kathy,

For May 1st it sure is cold. It is more like Dec 1st. We had snow to-day.

When I went on guard at 4:00 this morning it was really snowing. Now it has gotten a lot warmer and it has been raining.

I won't be able to write much this afternoon because I go on guard at 2:00 and am on till 4:00. I'll finish this letter after mail to-day. It seems like I get it every other day.

We got PX rations to-day and we got 5 cigars, five pack of gum, 12 candy bars.

I got in a poker game last night and lost $8.00, I got in another one this morning and lost about $1.50. I guess I am no poker player—I found that out. I should have sent that $10.00 to you like I said I would. I will do it next month, it will be a little late for Mothers Day but that is my own fault.

Well darling I am going to have to stop for now, I'll see you later.

Darling I received your April 24 letter to-night.

Tell your Grandma I wish her a Happy Birthday. How old is she? I am glad you got her a couple of dresses.

I am sorry I did not seem very cheerful in that one letter. You know how it is sometimes. I'll try and do better, now I feel a lot better. Things are very good now.

I forget, I also received a letter from Eleanor, a card saying the Nells are sending me the Readers Digest and two Enterprises.

Jan dear did you ever get that letter I wrote telling you that I broke my watch? If you didn't I'll tell you again.

One day (Just before Thanksgiving) we had fire mission we were all very busy getting ammo ready when one of the fellows threw a shell case and hit my watch and broke the crystal Now I've lost all the hands but one and it is in bad shape. It will run but the hands catch when I more my arm. So now it is not any good at all – till it gets fixed. I've been thinking about sending it home but as yet I have'nt done it I hate having it broke like that because I know how much you payed and how hard it was for you to pay for it. I still wear it.

Kathy really sounds very smart. I know she takes after you. That is one time I'll give you credit where it is due!

I guess Carl and I have our letter writing going OK now. I wrote to him last so I should be getting an ans one of these days.

I am glad mother is feeling better. I guess that job at Kingston was a little bit too much for her. I hope her new job is better.

Jan dear you do say so many swell things about me. I do love you so much for it. I am very very proud to call you "My Wife".

It turned out to be a very nice day it even warmed up so may be Spring will come now I hope.

I am out of news again—nothing new is it? We hear rumors that the Germans ask unconditional surrender this is a new rumor that last one just said Germans offered it to Am and English but this one says to all three. Who knows? I really don't think the end is very far off. I do hope it ends very soon.

After I finish your letter I am going to read my papers and a Life mag and then go to bed. I am very tired.

I was going to take a shower to-night but I'll wait till my laundry comes in I have some clean cloths coming.

I am wearing my bed room slippers now and boy do they fell swell almost like being home. If you were with me things would be perfect.

I really must get at my letter writing as soon as I get those stamps, I am now very far behind. People won't write to me if I keep this up.

Well kitten I believe this is about all I have for my report from Germany.

My dearest darling I do love and adore you with all my heart, soul and body.

God bless you and Kathy and may He keep you both safe from all harm.

My most sincere and deepest love and a million kisses.

Your Husband
Bill

May 1, 1945: Facts

~

Janet's Grandma was Margaret Marshman. She was born on April 25th, 1875.

Eleanor is Bill's cousin.

May 4, 1945
Somewhere in Germany

My Dearest Darling Janet and Kathy:

Good afternoon my darling. How is my one and only to-day?

It is a cloudy day this morning it was beautiful but got cloudy this afternoon. It started to rain a while ago. I guess just a shower.

I am on guard to-night, I don't know what time my first shift is. I've been getting guard every other day so that is'nt so bad.

I hope I get some mail from you to-night. I should, I did not get any last night.

This morning we got wed Stars and Stripes with big headlines "Hitler Dead", that is really swell news. I expect any day now to see it come to an end. I'll sure be glad, Then we will see that picture of the year-the point system on "are you still in or are you out"!

I have'nt mailed those letters I wrote yesterday. As yet I have'nt received the stamps.

We are having our March weather in May, the wind is really blowing now. It sure is good to be inside looking out at the rain. Just think I don't have to worry about the foxhole leaking or anything like that. This is the way I like it.

I should have you here to-morrow, I need my room moped up and you would be a swell one to do it. I believe you would enjoy that, would'nt you?

We hear that all the men that have 4 yrs or more service are going to be discharged. I guess they deserve it. I hope it is true, they have seen enough of the Army. I sure hope I don't have to be in 3-4 or 5 yrs.

We are having hamburgs to-night, that sure sounds good to me. I am hungry already. It is about 3:00 now. We have retreat at 4:30 and eat at 5:00.

I tried to get to bed early last night but it did'nt work. I had a very nice fire in my room so they came in and played poker. I read a while then fell asleep. I don't know what time I woke up but when I did no one was in the room so then I went to bed right and had a good nights sleep.

Well I think I'll stop for now, I'll be back later.

Back again, it is now 7:30 and we just had mail call. I received Kathy's letter to-night. I also received a letter from Jane and G.I. Extra. Your letter was dated April 26th.

That daughter of ours sure writes a cute letter. I like to hear from her. Don't you think she is kinda young for a boy friend? Ha!

Tell her I received the picture of her with out her cloths on (shame!). I want to save that picture, so when she gets to be 20 I can have some fun. I am a little devil are'nt I?

Of all the things to ask me-if I stick out in the places she and mummy do-what is that family of mine coming to? She asks more questions, we still have that book of knowledge don't we? I am going to need it I can see that!

Mother said she wanted to come down and spend a few days with you, before she went on her new job.

I do hope I'll soon stop touring Europe and start a tour of good old U.S.A. Well who knows maybe I'll be home one of these days-before long.

I go on guard at 10:00 to-night and finish at 12:00 noon to-morrow.

To-morrow at supper we are having champagne— from Gen "Ike" for our "meritorious service"

I think I write most of the time till I go on guard. I must write to Jean and Jane. I still did not receive the stamps yet so I am sending all your letter air mail collect, if you don't mind. I should get those stamps any day now. –Hold the phone. I borrowed 8 stamps. So I'll have stamps for this letter and to-morrows letter.

Sunday I should'nt have much to do so I am going to try and write you a dam long letter. My letters have been too dam short lately. I know you enjoy long letters and I do have the time. I can't seem to find enough things to say. I can fill pages and pages about how much I love you, you know that. There are so many things I would like to tell you but I can't—yet. Any how I'll try and write a long, long letter Sunday. I'll even tell you of some of my battle experiences, ones I have'nt told yet. I'll write anything to make it long.

Janet I still can't get over how wonderful you look. I sure did pick a beautiful girl. You should read the letter Jean and Eleanor write about you. They do think a lot of you. Jean said she hopes she can have the taste for furniture and fixing up a house like you do. They think you are just it. It sure is good to hear everyone say how wonderful you are. I sure hit the jack pot.

It has cleared off now, I suppose by morning it will be cloudy again. Fine weather.

Well kitten this looks like I've just about covered everything for my report from Germany for to-day.

My dearest Jan I do love and adore you with all my heart, soul and body.

God bless you and Kathy and may He keep you both safe from all harm.

My most sincere and deepest love and million kisses.

Your Husband,
Bill

May 5, 1945

Somewhere in Germany

My Dearest Darling Janet and Kathy:

I did not receive any mail from you to-day. I received two Enterprises—that was all.

Darling this war is just about over, in fact I look for it any time now. It sure is a wonderful felling to know that it is almost over. No worrying about getting shot at. I don't want to say too much till it is actually over-and then!

We have church at 1:00 to-morrow afternoon, so I guess I'll go this Sunday. I miss last Sunday but that was my own fault.

We had our Champagne for supper to-night and boy it was good. We also had some Bordeaux wine.

I suppose you wonder what we will do after the war—I wish I knew—I haven't even an idea. I just hope that we won't have to go to the Pacific. Well I guess we must trust in God, he knows best.

It is cloudy to-night, it looks like it will rain. I don't have to go on guard to-night. I am glad because I can get a good nights sleep.

I layed down this afternoon and slept most of the afternoon.

I wrote to Jean so now I am caught up on my letter writing. I'll ans them as I get them. It will be much simpler.

Gosh darling I do hope I'll be back in your arms before very long. What a wonderful day that will be. It hardly seems possible that the war is so near to the end. All these months of hell sure have'nt been in vain. I am very glad I've seen so much combat. I hope that is all the combat I see.

We have been talking about our past experiences and after you talk over some of the things we did you'd wonder how we ever came out alive. I have one story to tell you that I never mentioned before because I never wanted to worry you. It happened Sept 30th that day we were shelled for about 4 hrs. Janet I never thought I'd live through that shelling the shells were so close that dirt covered us. Art and I were in are uncovered fox hole, we held hands and I said the Lord's Prayer. They threw everything at us from 88mm to 150mm. After the shelling stopped we pulled back to a new position. I was so nervous that I could'nt hold a match still to light a cigarette. We were lucky no one was killed but we had several injured.

From that day on I knew God was watching over me. He had to be for anyone to come out of that alive. That is an experience I'll never forget. It is in my mind as if it happened only yesterday. I said I'd never tell you about it till the end of the war, so now you know.

One shell hit our gun and our fox hole was about 10ft from the gun. One fellow had dug a fox hole just one shovel deep and when the barrage started he didn't think the hole was deep enough to get in so he went in with some other fellows-lucky he did because his hole got a direct hit. He was only 5 ft from our hole, so you can see how close they were too us. I think the nearest one was 3 ft.

We have had a few shelling since but never like that, thank God.

I can sit and write about my combat experiences but one can ever have any idea what it is like till he is actually in combat. I never dreamed it was like it is, it is very hard to explain. Your dad knows what I mean, he went through the same thing. There are somethings that I've seen I'll never tell, I want to forget them. Somethings I can't forget. Even now many nights I still dream of combat and Lord how glad I am to wake up. It sure is relief to know that is only a dream. I suppose I'll be that way for quite sometime. I'll get over it. I have'nt been out of combat long enough to really forget it.

Art got a Grit to-day April 15, so I must read the late Berwick news. The Enterprises I got were March 24 and 29. To-morrow is Russian Day-Remember the Russians at home. I suppose dad will be with them to-morrow. The Russians are great people. We have a few around us and they sure do like the Americans.

There is a salt mine (it has'nt been used for a long time for mining salt) near us here and Janet the stuff that is stored down deep in the earth is amazing. They have more Ammo, clothing, cloth and hundreds of small items. Some of the fellows that have seen the stuff say they never saw any of it on a German soldier. Most of us think they were storing it for maybe the next war. I can't believe they would put clothing under the ground, ammo yes-but not clothing 2000 ft below the surface. Well we have it now, they can't use it now!

Darling how is our cute daughter doing these Spring days. I suppose seeing the flowers and all that will make her take notice now. Boy I can hardly waite to see her. I wonder if she will know her old man! (Ha). I do hope I'll be home for her birthday. Well we can hope, can't we?

Darling I guess this is about all I have for my report from Germany to-day.

My dearest darling I do love and adore you with all my heart, soul and body.

God bless you and Kathy and my He keep you both safe and sound from all harm.

My most sincere and deepest love and a million kisses.

Your Husband
Bill

May 6, 1945
Somewhere in Germany

My Dearest Darling Janet and Kathy,

What a rainy day, it is really coming down. It is now about 8:00 AM. I just finished breakfast so I thought I'd start my long letter to you, I did promise a long one to-day so I am going to try very hard.

I know one thing I am going to stay in as much as I can to-day-too wet! I am going to church at 1:00 I hope it won't be raining then.

Can CO is getting a book to-gether about our experiences in combat. I believe it will be very good. There will be maps and pictures and everything about our "travels".

Just 11 mo ago to-day the Invasions started. We sure have came a long way in 11 mo. (I mean the Am. Armies) As you know we hit combat July 9th, we went into position at dusk and 800 yrds from the enemy. I still was'nt frightened, I did'nt even give it much thought. I don't know why but I just knew I'd be alright.

The next morning we fired our first round into German postions, when I get home I'll tell you what I wrote on that first shell, a bit rough talk so I'd better not write it.

Things went along OK for a few days we still were'nt combat wise-yet. My fox hole was so flimsy that a BB shot could have went through it. A day or so later we moved our guns about 50 yds from our first positions, we have dug the gun in and was sitting around talking when "Bam" a shell hit back about 50 yds from us and about 5ft from the truck. I hit the ground and waited but no more came in, we went and looked at the truck, it had more holes than a sieve. I forgot to say I had just left the truck about 3 min before. You can see why I say the Good Lord has been watching over me.

Four days after that shell came in we moved into an anti-tank position 200 yrds below our last position. We had our gun in a sunkin road. The banks on each side of the road were about 12 ft high and the road was so narrow a truck could hardly get through. We stood guard on top of the hill, 25 yrds from the bank. This one day Stubbs, Mask and I were on the hill and we decided to see what was on the other side of some buildings there so we started, we had'nt gone far till Stubbs hit me and knocked me down—good thing because an 88mm shell landed on the other side of the barn. I judge we were about 30 ft from it, but a barn between us. Two landed close by after we thought is was safe we ran behind some more buildings we had'nt any more than got there when 3 came in, the shrapnel fell all around us. That was the last near shell that came in there while we were in that position.

All through that position snipers would take pop-shots at us. One German, I think was bound to get me. I went after some wood to build up my fox hole, the wood pile was behind a wagon shed and I had to pass over about 25 ft of open ground, the hedge row stopped to leave an opening into the orchard then there was a gate and from the gate ran a fence to this building. To-continue, I gathered a few logs and started back when "zing" a bullet kicked up the dust in front of me, back I went to the shed, I tried four times to get across that open space but each time he took a shot at me. So I waited—finally Sgt Johns came out and no one took a shot at him so I gathered my wood up and he and I took off to the guns.

All of this happened the first week of combat at St. Lo. There is so much to tell that I have just told the more important things, this is more of a outline, so save this letter and I'll be able to tell a few little things that happened that I have not put down here. I believe I have written you about a lot of the bombings and such while we were there. I never should have done that, you worried enough as it was. I think Sept 30, if you take note was the last letter I wrote on my experiences that shelling made me decide not to tell anything that happened to us, that would worry you. I won't attempt to cover all my travels, it would be impossible even to sit down and tell you everything from Omaha Beach to the Elbe would require many nights of patient listening. I am saving a lot of that to tell you in person. Each time that I have more time I relate a few of my experiences.

I have been more scared the last 3 mo of combat then I was in the beginning, I guess we knew what to expect after we had gone through 7 mo of it. We knew the Germans, their weapons and their tactics a lot better and to they were fighting harder than when we came across France. It does'nt take long to get battle wise. One shell—thats all!

Many a time we wondered to our selves—if we would come out of it alive. That is when the going gets rough. I am going to stop on the war subject for now. I'll pick it up in another letter. I think that is enough for one writing.

It is really raining now, boy I am glad I am inside.

It is now 10:00, I washed and shaved during the writing of this letter. The water I had on to heat got heated quicker than I thought it would.

Darling this sure would be a swell day for us to stay home, remember our Sundays that it rained how we layed around? This is really that kind of a Sunday. I don't think there were over 25 men to breakfast, most of them slept. I think I may lay down till dinner time, I feel a bit lazy myself.

I believe we are having chicken for dinner, that is what we had last Sunday.

Well Kitten I think I'll stop for now, I'll be back after church.

It is now 3:50, I did not go to church. It rained so hard that I did not go. We have to go about 8 mi and to ride in an open truck, I'd be soaked. I know I should have gone. I seem to find some excuse for not going. I did intend to go, Honest.

We did not have chicken for dinner, I guess we will have it for supper.

I am on guard to-night, I don't know what time I go on, I want to finish this letter before supper. If I get any mail from you to-night and have chance to write later, I will. I am afraid if I wait til the mail comes in I'll be on guard and not get a chance to finish the letter, so that is why I am going to finish it now.

I hope I get a lot of mail from you to-night, it seems like I get mail from you every other day. At least I get it. The mail lately have been coming very good. The best since I've been over here.

This is very crazy weather, it rained hard most of the afternoon and now the sun is trying to shine. I do hope warm weather soon comes, it's about time. How has it been at home? Has Spring really arrived?

It seems every time I try to write I get more guys in this room then Grand Central Station. I've got a nice warm room, so I guess that is why they come.

There was a movie this afternoon but I did not go, I slept for a while, then Stubbs came in and woke me up—Fine War!

Well darling it looks like there is a poker game getting started here so I'd better get away from my own table. Ha!

I hope I do get some mail from you to-night, I want to try another long one. I did do a little better than usual.

So I guess this is all I have for my report from Germany to-day.

My dearest darling I do love and adore you with all my heart, soul and body. May God bless you and Kathy and may He watch over you both and keep you from all harm.

My most sincere and deepest love and a million kisses.

Your Husband,
Bill

May 6, 1945: Facts

~

The Cannon Company book that William refers to in this letter was completed and published in Germany. The book was done by Jim Murdock with the help of other members of Cannon Company. It was titled "Cannon Company Cavalcade". I was able to obtain copies of the last few pages of this book from Cannon Company Veteran John Walsh. The pages list the Cannon Company roster and timeline during the war.

My grandfather's copy of this book was never located; however I was able to find the map from his book.

May 7, 1945
Somewhere in Germany

My Dearest Darling Janet and Kathy,

Darling <u>the War is Over!</u> Boy what a day this is. Thank God I've came through this one OK. It goes in to effect Tues at midnight but as far as that goes there is no more war. We have all day off—but being I'm on guard-guards always have been excused from all formations for 24 hrs.

It is 9:00 AM here now and 3:00 in Berwick-boy I bet they are really raising hell at home now. I'd give anything to see that.

The war ended 11 mo to the day that we hit France.

I bet you are very happy you can't be any happier than your husband. Now I hope I'll soon be home-to stay.

It still is hard to believe it is over, after all those months wishing and hoping and praying for it to be over and now it is. I hope all my praying to see you soon comes true. I have a feeling you will be seeing me before very long.

I'll be so dam glad to get home it won't be funny.

This is the first step toward our happiness, gosh darling it is so wonderful to have this war over.

I have to go on guard at 10:00 and it is almost that now. I did not receive any mail at all last night, I do hope I get some to-day.

I'll see you after dinner.

Back again. I have guard again to-night. Well I really don't mind it, it is'nt to bad.

I understand the states won't know about the war being over till Wed 12:01, in other words May 9 will be the real V-E day. Just 11 mo ago we went into combat.

We will soon be getting our new ETO uniforms, ribbons and everything. They say the E.T.O uniform is very nice. I'll tell you more about it when I see it.

It is a beautiful Spring day-a beautiful day for the war to be over which it is!

I just this minute saw a beautiful sight, 40 P47 flying in V formation went over us-Darling this is so wonderful I can't really believe it. Again I think I'll wake up and found out if is'nt true. How I wish I were with you now, we really would have a good time.

Again I must leave you for a while I want to go over to the boy who are making up the Cannon Co book, I have a few stories (true to) to tell them. I'll be back later.

Back again, I went and gave a few stories had a couple of drinks and then went and took a shower. I am kinda waiting for mail call before I finish this letter.

We had chicken for dinner to-day we did not have it like I thought we would yesterday.

I don't know what time I go on guard to-night, I hope I get the last shift, then I can write if I get any mail from you.

The Germans seem to be very well pleased that the

war is over. I think it is about time they are glad it is over.

It is almost time for supper in fact 15 min. I seem to write and run write and run. I'll get this letter written yet. I guess I am very restless to-day, can't blame me can you? I wonder what you are doing, I bet you are really happy. God bless you my darling, I do love you so very very much.

Well kitten I guess I'd better quit for now, I finish after supper.

I had supper and already pulled my first 2 hrs of guard. It is now 8:00

Darling I did not receive any mail from you again to-day. I do hope you are o.k. I do worry a bit when I don't get any letters for a couple of days.

It is a beautiful evening, so still and peaceful. You can smell the apple blossoms very strong to-night. Gosh Jan I do wish I were with you to-night. It is very warm to-night, a real spring evening.

I am so very anxious to know what happened at home when you heard the war was over. I bet you and dad were very happy. Now our next wonderful happening is me coming home to you.

Well we shall soon see that "movie of the year", all about this point system, I am really sweating that out. I did see in the S&S where combat troops, before going to the Pacific will go home for 21 days receive some training and then go to the Pacific. I hope I am one of the first home but never have to see the Pacific. So I am sweating that out also.

As I said before, I have'nt any idea what we will do now. I hope it is only one thing and that is that I see that famous skyline of New York before long.

I have two German metals, denoting years of service to the Wehmacht. I am sending you one in this letter and to-morrow I send you the other one . (12 yrs)

Red Dodson is making fun of my "up hill" writing, he gets a kick out of the way I write. He is some Red but a swell guy. He seems to have a swell girl friend she is always ask about Bill and Janet. She always asks how the baby is.

As yet I have'nt sent you that silk, I'd better get it sent, while I have time.

While I was on guard two Russian planes flew over, that is about 8 I've seen since I've been here.

I still didn't get my stamps so you'll have to receive some move letters air mail collect. I hope I soon get them.

There was an U.S.O show this evening but I could not go because I had guard. Oh Well maybe another time.

I suppose now we won't have to have blackout curtains on the window, I hope they even turn on street lights-boy that will be something.

Well darling I guess this is about all I have for my report from Germany to-day.

My dearest Janet I do love and adore you with all my

heart, soul and body. God bless you and Kathy and may he keep you both safe from all harm. My most sincere and deepest love and a million kisses.

Your Husband,
Bill

May 9, 1945
Somewhere in Germany

My Dearest Darling Janet and Kathy,

Good afternoon darling. Gosh it is another beautiful day.

I am writing this letter in my room and I have one of the two big windows open. There is a gentle warm breeze blowing. It is truly a spring day.

We took a hike this morning, about 8 miles. It was like leafing through the pages of a geography book. The windmills, farmers in the field, canals and quaint villages all bring back the days I use to study about Germany.

We are in a very pretty part of Germany. I suppose another reason things look so beautiful is because the war is over, that sure makes a big difference.

I have guard to-night, my first shift is from 6 to 8 so that is'nt so bad. I'll be able to continue this letter till I see if I receive any mail from you.

I'll have to leave you already, they want some ball players, so here I go!

I just ate supper and I'll soon have to go o guard. We had a very good baseball game this afternoon. The side I was on won 18-16. We even had to play two extra innings.

I am going to try and look up Geo, B. this week. One

of our officers is going to find out where he is and if he can find him he will find transportation to see him.

I saw 4 more Russian planes to-day. They were American made Liberators but had the Red Star.

Gosh kitten I do hope I get some mail from you to-night, I'll soon find out very soon.

I'll be dam, I am on guard at 8:00 to 10:00 instead of 6–8. So I guess I'll have to finish this letter now because after 10:00 I won't have a chance to write.

I've been thinking a lot of you to-day darling. I am so anxious to get back to you but it may be a long while. They say it will take a while to get us home-if we don't have to go to the Pacific, Oh well things might work out OK. I am not worrying. When we see this picture we will know a lot more.

We hear we will get furloughs home, I don't know how true it is. Some of the boys (2) are going Riveria (?) this week. Two are going to Paris. By gosh I should get a pass to someplace sometime. Well maybe I'll be first in furloughs home!!!

How's my daughter? I bet she is really big, you'll have to send me some more pictures of her. I need some more paper as you can see, I am using this still paper.

Last night I stay up till 11:30 and listened to the radio. There was a lot of good music on. I really enjoyed myself. I was the only one in the room so I turned out the light lit my pipe, wished I had you on my lap, and settled down to some good music. Last night I miss you more than I have since I've been over here. Being the end of the war, alone and American music—all of that brought on this loneliness.

Darling I do love you so very much, I miss you so very much. I long to be held in you arms. I do hope God grants me an early return to you my dearest.

Well kitten I guess this is all I have for my report from Germany to-day.

My dearest darling I do love and adore you with all my heart, soul and body.

God bless you and Kathy and may he keep you both safe and sound from all harm.

My most sincere and deepest love and a million kisses.

Your husband
Bill

May 12, 1945
Somewhere in Germany

My Dearest Darling Janet and Kathy,

Darling I did not receive any mail from you to-day. My last letter from you was April 27. I hope I get a letter from you to-morrow. To-day I have been overseas one year, gosh it seems longer. It has been over a year since I last saw you and I do miss you so very much.

Last night I sent you and Jane some German insignias. I knew I'd have to send them in a separate envelope because it would be too heavy if I didn't. I sent the Marshmans some of the things also mother and Rosebud. I wrote a letter to Marshmans.

It has been really hot to-day, London just reported 85 degrees, five degrees hotter than yesterday.

It also was reported over the radio this afternoon that Gen "Ike" said he did not want any troops to go to the Pacific that had fought in the campaigns over here. The announcer said he (Gen E.) usually gets what he wants. I sure hope so. Well time will tell!

We were told what courses we could take in this Educational Program. They are Farm, Business, technical and another one I have forgotten. Under each of those headings are two to five subjects that can be taken. I want to take the business course. We will know more about it next week.

Well I did get an Enterprise April 12th. I saw in the Enterprise I got the other day it told a little about the 35th. Do you ever see anything about us? You never mention it if you do.

To-morrow (Sunday) I have K.P. I hope I can get off for church. I am going to try anyway.

Janet I wish you could see this part of Germany I am in, it is really beautiful. I tell you so much about it, you may be getting tired of hearing it, but there is really beautiful scenery here.

I suppose there will be some good music on the radio to-night. I want to go to bed early, I say that every time I have a night off but never do it. I wish I could hear the Hit Parade, I'd give anything to hear that. It has been so long since I did hear it.

I don't have any important news, I hope we soon find out what we are going to do. I guess we will have to sit tight. I just put on my civilian shoes boy do they feel good. Getting in practice!

Gosh kitten these night remind me of our H.S days. Remember the dances, plays and all that during the end of school-in our Jr and Sr year. Well your Jr and Sr year anyway. This brings back the nights I use to take you home, those warm, moon lite nights and you always looking so beautiful. How I'd love to be with you now. This would be a swell evening for a ride in the country.

Janet dear I am madly in love with you, I do think about you so much, I just long to hold you in my arms and smother you with kisses.

I pray to God it won't be long now till I'll be with you and Kathy. I am so very anxious to see Kathy I don't know what to do. Do you think she would like to see her "old man"?!! Ha!

I've been wondering about Bill. I wonder if he had his last exam. I do hope he doesn't have to go. I know Sis wouldn't take it like you have. Again it might make a woman out of her. If he does go in I don't think he'll every see any fighting-Remember what they all said about me? Here I am with 3 campaign stars!!!

Your Grandfather ask me not to forget the proposition they put to me-about you and I staying at Blythyhems while they go for a vacation. I hope I can soon do that, don't you?

Well kitten I guess I've just about covered everything in my report from Germany to-day.

My darling wife I do love and adore you with all my heart, soul and body.

God bless you and Kathy and may he keep you both safe from all harm.

My most sincere and deepest love and a million kisses.

Your Husband,
Bill

May 16, 1945
Somewhere in Germany

My Dearest Darling Janet and Kathy,

It is now 5:45 PM. I thought I start a letter to you before I went to work on the book. I don't have much news but I will try and make this as long as I can.

I am sending you the Special Edition of Santa Fe Express. I think you will enjoy it. Most of the items are from the news paper back home. You can see we did have a little publicity.

It is a beautiful day a little breeze blowing but just enough to keep it cool.

If after to-morrow you don't hear from me for a couple of days don't worry. I'll be ok but I can't tell you anything about it. I hope you don't worry about me so much now-there is'nt a war over here now, you know!

I do hope I get some mail from you to-night, then I'll be able to write a long letter.

Darling I am going to stop now, I'll be back later to-night.

Here I am back already we just had mail call. I got one letter and that was from Jean, it was written on V-E Day. I am very anxious to hear from you and what you did on V-E Day.

I think I'll go to the movies to-night. There is a movie

at the Hospital to-night "Two Yanks Abroad", it sounds good. I've been working all day, so I think I'll quit for to-night. The show does'nt start till 8:00.

Darn it this looks like it might be a short letter again to-night, I do hate it because my letters are so short.

It seems so strange not to hear a lot of war news. We hear very little of Pacific news. In fact I don't care to hear anything about the Pacific. Ha!

Gosh darling, I do love you so very much, and boy do I miss you. Since the war is over, I think it is a lot worse. When the war was on I kinda had my mind occupied! But now all any of us think about is home. I do hope I will get home soon, but I really don't look for it for quite some time. I quess we might as well face the facts. I do hope I am wrong and that I get home before long.

As yet I have'nt heard anything about our new uniforms we should be getting them soon.

Cn Co. played the med this afternoon and we beat them 5–4. It was a good game—I guess, I did not see it because I was working. The nurses were there to!! There is 6 of them now, Americans to!!

I wonder what it feels like to kiss a girl, you were the last girl I kissed. (Harrisburg-remember?) You see I've been a good boy—honest!

Well kitten I must leave you now. This is all I have for my report from Germany to-day.

My dearest Janet I do love and adore you with all my

heart, soul and body.

May God bless you and Kathy and may He keep you both from all harm.

My most sincere and deepest love and a million kisses.

Your husband,
Bill

May 18, 1945
Lunhne, Germany

My Dearest Darling Janet and Kathy,

I thought I'd write to you this afternoon and then if I received any mail I'd ans it later to-night.

This morning I wrote to Jane, I still have Jean's letter ans. I may write that later.

The picture I saw last night was "The Hairy Ape" with Tom Bendix. It was'nt bad, I did enjoy it. The night before I also saw Tom Bendix play. I suppose there will be a movie to-night if there is I guess I'll go.

We had a very hard thunder storm, In fact it knocked down (lightening struck it) the flag pole that was along side the building we saw the movie in last night. The rain came down in sheets and the lightning was very heavy. It sounded like the war was on again, all the cracking and the thunder. To-day it is cloudy and looks like rain.

This morning I sent you V-E Day S&S. I believe you will like it.

We had liver for dinner and I do eat it, so you see I have change a little.

Jan is'nt Dad's birthday Sunday, 20th? I know it is very near and I thought it was 20th I believe I am right. Jane's is to-day is'nt it? I am not very good at remembering dates that is some dates!

We were going to have a ball game this afternoon but it is to wet, so I guess we will take it easy all day.

Is Frank C. still friends with that fellow from Wash? I hope he is maybe we could use his help again. He was willing to do something before so maybe again!

I can see now this is not going to be a very long letter. I hope I get some mail to-night then I'll be able to write again.

Well kitten I guess I'll close now. So this is all I have for my report from Germany to-day.

My dearest Jan. I do love and adore you with all my heart, soul and body.

God bless you and Kathy and may He keep you both safe from all harm.

My most sincere and deepest love and million kisses.

Your Husband
Bill

May 24 , 1945
Rinkerode, Germany

My Dearest Darling Janet and Kathy,

Well no mail from you to-night. I got 1 Enterprise and the Vet Mag.-that's all. I can't kick very few got any mail.

I wrote to mother and Jean to-day. Now that is off my mind.

As usual I worked all day on the book. It really will be a swell book when it is finished.

False alarm-as yet we do not have those other battle stars. So so far only 60 pts. We heard one strong rumor that all men with 60 to 85 pts would be A of A—just a rumor, so far nothing to it. There should be plenty of rumors now. There always are in this Div—sometimes some of them have hair on—I mean they come true.

It has been partly cloudy all day but now 7:25 it is clearing off very nice.

We are suppose to get our E.T.O. jackets in a day or two. I guess I did tell you that before.

Darling how are you feeling? Gosh I do hope you are OK, If only you could get your nerves settled. I know you've been a brave girl for so long and it has been too much for you.

I hope that soon that neither one of us will have to worry about each other. I hope we will soon be with each other—never to part again. Boy after the Japs give up(?) and I get home, hell and high water won't be able to drag me away from you. Gosh Janet I miss you so very much. I'd give a million dollars to see you right now. Well maybe, who knows, I might see you before long.

Things are very dull here, this town we are in just a little place. Even if it was as big as N.Y. we still would'nt have any more excitement because we can't go in the town anyhow.

The mayor of the Rinkerode was once a member of the German Congress. He said he voted against Hitler was then sent back as Mayor of Rinkerode, finally thrown out because of his lack of help with the Nazis. He was to be taken to a concentration camp but because of the bombings he was never taken. He says the German people are to blame, they knew what was going on. Now he says that they all must help the Americans and help Germany build up a democracy. The Germans so far have bend over backward to help us. Here might explain why. Hitler and Gobels told the German people that the Americans would kill the men, rape the women and burn their houses. When the Americans came, they were so scared then and so taken back that the Americans did'nt do anything, that now they do most anything the Americans ask. I tell you these things because I think they might interest you. To tell you the truth I can't quite figure the Germans out, they seem very strange. Maybe it is the way they have been raised!!!

We had a dam good peach pie to-day. We give the German bakery the stuff and he bakes it for us. This is the third time we have had pie since we have been here. I was going to tell you about it before but forgot it. One track mind!

Dina Shore is singing "I Walk Alone"—true how true!

It is now 8:00—News just said Himler committed suicide yesterday. Tough S___.

It does'nt get dark here till about 10:30. I guess it will be like England last summer-Gosh I've come a long way since last June. From England to within 45 mi of Berlin. I get around!

I guess that is something else I did not tell you and that was I was dam close to Berlin—I think we got the closest of any American unit. When we were near Berlin we were not with the Div we were attached to the 83 Div. I sent you a circular on it last week.

Well kitten I guess your husband has just about completed his report from Germany to-day.

My dearest darling wife I do love and adore you with all of my heart, soul and body.

God Bless you and Kathy and may He keep you both safe from all harm. My most sincere and deepest love and a million kisses.

Your Husband
To my wife x x x x x x x x x x x x x
To Kathy x x x x x x x x x x x x

May 24, 1945: Photos

~

Bill wrote on the back of the photo: "Elbe River near Barby where the 35th was 42 miles from Berlin!"

June 11, 1945
Koblenz, Germany

I did not receive any mail from you to-day. I received a letter from Foster and he is near Schweinfurt Ger. I've spend ½ hr look for that place but I can't find it. I'll have to write and tell him where I am and to give me more detailed lay of the land.

We had quite a bit of rain to-day but around 6:00 this evening it cleared up.

I do not have guard to-night but I expect it to-morrow. I have been getting it every other day. One day they missed me and I got two days off. I doubt if that will happen again.

I got a shave and a hair cut to-day all for two cigarettes!

I understand that we soon will have three day passes to Luxembourg City. I hope to get one of those.

I have'nt much news to-day not much has happened.

We have quite a sports program, I am going out for volley ball-that is if they have enough men interested.

As yet I don't know when we will start those courses I told you about, I hope soon.

I think after I finish this letter to you I'll do my nightly reading. I have one mag to read yet.

I should write to Foster to-night but maybe I'll wait till to-morrow.

Gee kitten I do miss you so much. We don't do much and it sure give a guy a lot of time to think about home. Well I guess I'll have to think for a while. At least I have some beautiful memories and I know I'll have a very bright future.

As yet I have'nt received my envelopes so I'll have to send this A.M. collect. If you don't mind.

I don't even know any good rumors to night.

It is so nice and peaceful now. Outside the birds are singing so sweetly and there is a warm fresh breeze blowing in thru our two windows. Once in a while some one will do down to hall whistling a popular tune. That is the way things stand as of now at our little camp on the River Rhine.

I believe our book will be published in a very few weeks, so maybe in a month we will get them. I am very anxious for you to read it. I am getting "Sammy" a copy too, I thought maybe he would enjoy it. Jane also wants one. It will have over a hundred pages so far.

Well kitten this sure is a short letter to-night I know you understand why. When I don't receive any mail it is hard to write. I know you find it the same way.

So I guess this is all I have for my report from Germany to-day.

My dearest darling Jan I do love you and adore you so very much.

God bless you and Kathy and may He keep you both

safe from all harm.

My most sincere and deepest love and a million kisses.

Your Husband
Bill

PS To my beautiful wife xxxxxxxxxxxxxx
To Kathy xxxxxxxxxx

June 18, 1945
Koblenz, Germany

My Dearest Darling Janet and Kathy,

Hi my darling! I am back again after three swell days in Luxembourg. I got back last night and when I arrived I was handed four letters from you. They were 5x7 two beautiful fathers day cards. Oh darling the fathers day card you sent me was beautiful. Your beautiful darling.

First I am going to ans your letters then tell you about my trip.

Gee Jan that box sounds swell even blackberry wine boy I can hardly wait. I like camels very well, in fact you should see the cigarettes I have now, I have two cartons and 4 PKs. We got a weeks ration in Luxembourg.

Kitten I want you to drag me all over and show me off because I can show you off at the same time. I sure do miss you darling.

Why did I have to marry a (Englishman) you asked me so here goes- A—H----is "Assholes" I know it is a strange word but very descriptive don't you think!!??!!

So you think you are going to torment me, well don't forget your husband has been fighting man and he might just out of meanness take so much and he might carry you upstairs and boy the sparks will fly.

I haven't heard from Geo C. for quite some time. I've

been wondering about him myself. I hope I hear from him soon.

I hope Dad gets to feeling better, I know how he is when he gets sick.

So my (our) daughter is spoiled, my dear how do you expect me to break her way over here. I must say Jan that slapping you in the face should stop don't let that get to far. I wish I was home, I suppose I'd be just as bad. I hope something can be done about that. I don't like that at all. Please Kitten don't wait til I get home to stop it because it maybe many months til I arrive on the scene. I know you are doing a good job and I wish above all that I could be there and take some of that burden off of your hands.

Thanks Darling for the cartons. I know Bill Mauldine quit well-who wouldn't being a infantryman. I don't know him personally, but I know his cartons. I am going to hang the cartons up on my locker wall. Thanks again. Oh, I also saw that picture of the guys at the induction center, It sure brought back memories—Aug 3 !!

I am glad you are reading Mauldine's "Up Front" It gives a swell picture of what the Inf goes through. Oh though I didn't get the Hell the line boys got, you must understand that. There has been something that I wanted to say about how I wanted to be treated when I come home-as long as we are on the subject of combat-so here goes.

I know you, Dad, in fact everyone is anxious to know

what different things felt like, how I felt in combat, when a bomb fell, or when we all had to fight the weather. I think maybe you will wonder if you should ask about such things-yes by all means. What I went through is in the past, it doesn't bother me anymore. I want you to ask all the questions you can think of. Ask them just like I had been on a trip-you how you always get everything out of me.

Greatest of all I don't want to be babied-I am a grown up man, I fought a war, I want everyone to act natural-no fuss. You know over here we had no time for weaklings and babies-so please treat me like you did before I came in the Army-that way is a beautiful way to be treated. When I come home (whenever that is) I'll tell you what I mean-maybe I haven't made myself very clear. I hope I have.

Tell Kathy her daddy thanks her for the card and five dollars. I sure have a swell family-God Bless them. Kitten the card you sent me was really beautiful. Darling how much I love you-you are all such a perfect wife.

Now to start on "my trip". I really had a swell time. I'll start at the beginning.

I left the company wed eve at 6:15 stayed at Sv Co all night. During my stay there I spent a couple of hours with C.B Thompson, he asked all about you and I showed him pictures you sent me.

We left SV Company at 6:30 Thrusday morning. Jan

the scenery was beautiful, we went along the Mosele River for quite a ways. All along the river on both sides were vineyards. I never saw so many my whole life. Here in this valley is where the famous Mosele Wine comes from. The vineyards are on the sides of the hills-steep hills too. I don't see how they stand up to pick the grapes. All during my trip I wishing you were with me. I know how much you would have enjoyed it. We pasted by many old towns and many old castles. We arrived in a city Esch, 12 mi from Luxembourg City. We then got our passes and PX cards, were assigned our room, then went to dinner. There are two buildings. The are called Grand Hotel and G.H. Anex. I was in the G.H. Anex five blocks from the main building. In the main building is were we ate and saw the movies and also got our money changed. The meals were swell and the girls served us-even keep our cups filled up with coffee-girls!! I saw a USO show it was quite good-in fact I went back the next night and saw it over again. I saw quite a few movies. I saw a "Tree grows in Brooklyn", "Mrs Pinkerton", "Cinderella (?) Jones" (In this picture the girl said she was born in Wilkes-Barre PA, June 18, 1921, in fact they talked about WB quite often. The girl was Joan Leslie). "The Mark of the Whistler". Then there was another one-I got in at the middle and I never did find out what the name of it was. So you can see I spent quite a bit of time at the shows. One morning I went shopping I bought you three things two is for mothers day and the other is because I love you so much and miss you so. Boy I am going to make you suffer, I am not telling you what I am sending you. I am quite sure you will love all three-if fact two are the same.

Your passes were good for three days and you could be out all night if you wanted to. Me I was usually in bed by 11:30. I never got up for breakfast only Sunday morning. They had a dance one night, in fact it was Thrusday night, I went just to watch.

I met a young fellow from Cleveland OH. He and I went around together-I wasn't looking for women or anything like that. I was enjoying myself in my own way. I bought seven postcards pics Lux City and four of Esch. I also bought a booklet "Do you know Luxembourg".

Luxembourg City is really old. You can see that by the postcards. It really is wonderful to see these ancient towns that we use to read about.

During my stay there I read quite a bit waiting for dinner or a show. The library was across the hill from the theater.

The hardest thing for me was to be without you. I was very glad to get back because I missed writing to you. It seems I talk to you everyday. I never knew it meant so much to me, til I was away from my writing to you for three days I would go nuts if I couldn't write to you.

You should see the kids that follow you and ask for chewing gum or candy. Just little fellows too. I gave all my chewing gum away. They sure do like it. A lot of the kids were little blond haired girls, One I remember very well she was about two and another little kid with her must have been around 4, the one 4 asked for chewing gum so I gave both of them a stick. The little tot 2, just looked up at me and smiled but never said a word but that smile said "Thanks". Very many people speak English in fact most of the girls that served us spoke English.

We went into a bookstore (where I bought the booklet on Lux) and there the women spoke swell English. We asked her about the German occupation. She said they were fined 50 F. ($1.00) for speaking French. They could speak English but no French, they wanted them to speak German. She said since they were not allowed to speak French they greeted the Germans morning, noon or night with "good morning" that made them mad. The Germans told them they would not take their men away and she said they not only took them for slave labor but for the Army. She was very interesting. She said it seemed very strange to go where you please after 4 years of Iron rule.

It was very cool during our stay there but Sunday when we left it was a very beautiful day. It took us 5 hours by truck—open trucks at that.

That is about all there is to tell about the trip because I didn't really do anything special I just took it easy. The beer and wine was quite good!!

We also were issued a booklet called "Attack" it is

all about the 35th. I am sending that in another evelope. I have put some lines under some of things I don't want you to miss. Note the first page in the book-interesting!!

I am going out for volleyball this morning—at 10:00. I believe it is 10:00.

The boys tell me we know have champagne-boy we drink that here like it was just so much water. Fine place to live!

Janet dear how much I miss you, Gosh kitten I just love you more and more each day. Sometimes I think I can't stand it any longer—but I must. Everytime I see some girl with really black hair how I think of you. So many little things I remember about you. I just want to hold you in my arms and tell you how much I adore you. I hope before long darling we will be together.

Well darling, I hate to stop now but I must get my things fixed up. I have to get some clothes pressed and my locker back in shape after three days it is in bad shape. If I get any mail tonight I'll write again-I expect guard tonight. So I guess this is all I have from my report from Germany today.

My dearest Janet I do love you with all my heart soul and body. God bless you my darling and may he keep you and Kathy all safe from all harm. My most sincere and deepest love and a million kisses.

Your Husband—*William!*

PS I adore you Jan xxxxxxxxxxxxxxxxx Bill.

I went down to the mail clerks and he handed me a letter from you dated June 8th so I will answer it later today. Love Bill

June 18, 1945: Photos and Facts

~

The booklet that was purchased in Luxembourg was titled *Do you know Luxembourg?* The book is dedicated "To our friend the allied soldier". The back cover states the following:

"...that is your friends' country and people: The charming Luxembourg. May be these few pictures make you realize the love of Luxembourgers for their country and their thankfulness to those who restored them to what the pictures showed: Their land, their people, their freedom, their religion and their throne." (Text by Gusty Muller. Published by St. Pauls Printing House, Luxembourg, 1945.)

I was fortunate to get in touch with Patrick Beck from Baschleiden, Luxembourg. He is a reenactor with 35th Infantry Division Association Luxembourg, also known as "The 7th Company". Baschleiden is a town that Cannon Company helped liberate during the Battle of the

Bulge. I sent him a few of my grandfather's photos and copies of postcards from his collection. Patrick responded to me with the email below:

Hi Beth,

Many, many,many thanks for your postcards, they are great and so very interesting to me.

I do recognize all the places and they are indeed in the towns quoted on the cards.

At least one of them has been taken during the occupation 1940-1944 (ESCH) there is a German soldier on it riding a bicycle.

ESCH also called ESCH-SUR-ALZETTE is in the south of the country and former industrial centre with many steel mills...

LUXEMBOURG is the main city of our country.

The Moselle runs in the South-East and does the frontier between Germany and Luxembourg, along the Moselle river they still produce wine (mainly white wine).

It's funny the story your Grandpa wrote on the cards as that story reflects indeed a lot of what went on during these bitter times in Luxembourg.

Indeed during the war the Germans made the people to change the (mostly) in French Names of the villages, streets, avenues... into German, they even changed their first names

BAUSCHELT (lux.) or BOULAIDE (Fr.) would be

BAUSCHLEIDEN

e.g a person called HENRI (=Henry) was to be called HEINRICH (=Henry)

or a ANNE would be ANNA, a JOSEPH -> JOSEF and so on...

Many men and women were forced to go to Germany and work in the factories or on the farms...

My uncle was withdrawn for working for the Germans (building trenches and other military artifacts in Poland—1944),they took him just a few months before the liberation by the Americans. Fortunately he made it back in July 1945. I have copies of the letters he wrote home to his parents and brothers...many of these letters were written in German—otherwise they would have failed the German censorship! In 1945 he ended up as a POW in a US POW-camp and passed some time there before he was "recognized" as being not a German soldier but forced withdrawn Luxembourger.

On August 1942 the Germans decided to withdraw young men from Luxembourg into the "Wehrmacht" (their army).

Upon this on August 31st 1942—Luxembourg lay down its work and went on a "general strike" all over the country in order to show that the people would not agree with the nazi's decision.

Farmer preferred to pour the milk into the sink than deliver it to the dairies, steel workers, teachers,... lay down their work and went home...

The Nazis were very surprised by this and during the war no other country did such to them...

Immediately they took severe actions and a number of people were shoot and their families had to leave their homes and were sent to Germany or other occupied countries and their homes were given to Germans or German friendly people. On the other hand there were also Luxembourger Nazis who wanted the Luxembourgers to become German.

So long for a little bit of Luxembourg in WW2, I hope I didn't bore you too much with all of this...

Thanks again for your sharing—I can surely use this for one of my group's future exhibition. Greetings, Patrick.

One of the postcards that was copied and sent to Patrick to identify.

June 27, 1945
Koblenz, Germany

My Dearest Darling Janet and Kathy,

It is now 5:00, so I thought I'd write a bit before supper. I don't believe we will have retreat—I know we won't the flag is'nt up and besides it has been raining a little bit.

Janet, I saw a crazy movie this after-noon it was Laurel and Hardy in "Bullfighters", I laughed till I hurt. There was also a sport picture, news reel and a short called "I won't play." It was a very enjoyable afternoon.

I went out to watch the 320th and 137 play ball but it started to rain so I came in, 320th was ahead when I left.

I believe I told you before the 320 baseball team is staying here with us, because they are using our ball field. I think the proper name for Cn. Co. barracks would be "Cannon Hotel" or "Hotel Cannon" we now are feeding about 200 men. Our little Co of 113 men sure has grown.

I am on guard to-night—third shift 10–12 at the jail. I stay there all the time till my last shift at 6:00 to-morrow eve. I sleep there also. It is'nt bad, it is in side and we can write or read. I think I'll do both to-night. I don't leave till 10:00 so I'll get some writing done here before I go.

I hope I get some mail from you to-night, my darling.

Last night Raymond Carroll and I had the fellows just about crazy. For some reason or other the light on our room would not work and we wanted to read. We decided to read to each other, (his bed is across the room from mine) so we started to read "Sleep no More" a collection of horror stories. He read two and then I started another one. We started to read at 11:00 and quit just before 12:00—they did'nt say anything last night but this morning they raised Hell (in fun). We told them that if we had stopped in the middle of any of those stories—all three of them would have been mad. We have a good bunch here we get along fine, and we are always kidding one another.

While I was writing that last line they called chow—so out I went hell bent—trying not to be the 199th in line—I made it ok!!

I just received a very sweet letter from a very sweet girl—her name is Janet—that really is a lovely name, don't you think?

I'll be looking for the box now, I can tell you now I'll enjoy every bit of it. I always love the boxes you send me.

I don't wear the broken watch any more I keep it in my locker—you don't mind do you?

Darling when I am discharge from the army you may personally buy me a watch, I'll go with you to the bank, draw out $200 (?) and go to Shermans or someplace and I'll stand out side while you buy it. Now how's that? Pretty good plan is'nt?

You sure did sound devilish when you wrote that June 20 letter, you are again like my Janet. Oh gosh kitten how I love you.

And Mrs. M.W. G. just because I used red ink does'nt mean anything—I don't believe it does! By gosh when I get home you'll think your in a certain business—I don't mean maybe! I like to hear you talk like that—after all we are married and you are a woman and you (me too) have been away from it for quite some time—Have'nt you??!!-Only kidding, honest about "Have'nt you". I don't think you are awful because I love you and you are my wife. I kissed the kiss you sent me but I could'nt even taste the brand-little heavier next time—please!

I think I'll go over to the jail, about 8:00 I want to find out where I sleep and maybe I'll go to the Regt band concert at the Italian Camp. I understand at that guard we can read and play cards. That's the place for me—easy like.

I am kinda glad I don't have a guard post out side to-night, It kinda looks like rain—In fact right now it really is coming down. Just started.

I was going out to see "Aunt Mary" but it is raining too hard. As yet our toilets are not working here in the barracks. We are getting the hot water system fixed now. I suppose when we get everything all fixed up nice—we'll move. We are in French territory anyhow. So far we have'nt been in our territory. We were in Russian, English and now French—Line Army of Occupation.

I only have a few envelopes left now, so I went and

ordered 32 more. I have a lot of plain envelopes so I'll send some of your letters collect – if you don't mind. I don't want to send any "collect" letters to anyone else but you—I guess it would'nt be right and I know you understand.

I am very anxious for you to receive the picture I sent you, I do hope you like it. I am looking for a nice big picture of my sweetheart—one I can pin-up on the wall by my bed. I am very much in love with that pin-up girl here name—"Janet"—do you know her? She has beautiful jet black hair, her eyes, gosh there clear out of this world and her shape well you can't keep your hands off of those dangerous curves. Her lips are so soft and when you kiss her she really means it, her kisses make every muscle tighten and every nerve strain. Just to look at her makes your heart best faster and faster. Now do you doubt that I am in love you my dear? Janet darling I mean every word of that simple description of you.

Well my darling wife I guess this is about all I have for My Report from Germany to-night.

My dearest Kitten I do love and adore you with all my heart, soul and body.

God bless you my sweet and may He watch over you and Kathy and keep you both from all harm.

My most sincere and deepest love and a million kisses.

Your Husband, *Bill*

PS

I love you

PSS

I adore you

Xxxxxxxxxx

Xxxxxxxxxx

Xxxxxxxxxx for my two girls

June 27, 1945: Photos and Facts

~

Photo from Bill's collection taken at Koblenz. He wrote on the back: "Part of Koblenz it all looks like this."

July 9, 1945

Koblenz, Germany
9:50 AM

My Dearest Darling Janet and Kathy,

It is a beautiful July morning, there isn't a cloud in the sky. I do believe we are going to have some summer after all. I hope.

Well I am still alone in the supply room. We all believe the supply Sgt went to Strasebourg with the Cannons, although he did not tell anyone he was going. So far I have'nt run up against anything I can't really handle—I hope I don't.

Honey I don't believe we are moving tomorrow. I hear it will be the 12th so I suppose it will be sometime this week. I sure hope the Army don't screw up & change it's mind & make us stay here. I'll be glad when I see N.Y. or any other A.M. port then I'll be really sure.

Rumor also has it men under 50 pts will be transferred out of the Div & all above 50–80 will be kept in the Div & we will go into reserve back in the states. Rumor also has it our base camp will be a Camp Roberts Calif. All of this is just rumors, we probably won't know til we get home where our base camp will be.

I wrote to mother this morning & told her the news, I bet she'll be glad.

So far this morning I haven't much news. I told you all of it in last nights letter. I'll keep this letter going all day. I haven't been very busy this morning. I hope it stays that way all day. I am lazy myself!

The French are taking over our D.P. camp they have moved in along side of us. They first 1,000 Italians left today for Italy. I bet they are a happy bunch of boys. I know just how they feel. We have polish boys working for us now. They are all the same, hard to find when there is work to be done. But when it comes to work who isn't hard to find-American, Polish, Russian, Italian there all the same.

Ah I see the S&S is in. I must go and see if there is anything in about the 35th leaving. See you later kitten!

It is now 6:45 I just finished washing and shaving.

To-night kitten I received the box you send me. Boy that blackberry wine was swell, it's all gone now. I sure did enjoy it. Thanks for the paper, hankerchiefs, deviled ham, cigars and tobacco & cigarettes. Now I have 3 full cartons. The tobacco comes in handy I haven't had any pipe tobacco for over a week. Thanks for everything Darling. I love you.

I received 4 July 1st letter to-night. I also received a letter from Jean.

Darling I hope it won't be very many weeks that you & I will be sitting on the back porch of grandma's. Oh Darling what a wonderful 30 days that will be. It will be heaven in every sense of the word.

Kitten I know you can't write everyday, I understand very well, don't worry about it.

July 1st it was very cool here and there you suffered from the heat-what a place we are in here.

So are daughter is acting up again? Well we must stop that, I want her to be a lady and not a child every one will talk about-in the wrong way. I don't understand Bob, I wish sis would take more time with him. There is an example of neglecting a child, I don't want that to happen to Kathy. We must spend as much time with her as possible-we must. I don't think a spanking hurts her at all, she old enough now to know what it is for. I believe in them very much.

Jan I am so very glad you and I have such a very strong love, I don't know what I I'd every do with out you. You are so wonderful. I am glad you are proud of me, that is what I want you to be.

The reason I never mention Art very much is that he is in another room and I don't see him very often and at the present he is on pass to the riveria. We haven't had any quarrel we are still the best of friends.

I'll be very anxious to get Kathy's picture. I can hardly waite for yours—you darling.

I sure had my hands full this afternoon. At 11:30 they told me to get all they coke bottles gathered up and take them to Sv. Co. so I ran upstairs downstairs over to the

Italian and Polish camps and finally policed up twenty cases. I took them to Sv. Co. got the rations (eats) and a big box full of games. I had to go to Regt for the 1st Sgt. I had full after noon. When I got back they brought in 3 full cases of empty bottles. I was mad but it did not do me any good, so we still have them. The Supply Sgt game back this evening. He had been in Strasebourg with the guns.

I've been on the go all day and I am going to take it easy. I am kinda tried to-night.

Darling, I don't have anymore news, so I guess this is all I have for my report from Germany to day.

My dearest Janet I do love and adore you with all my heart, soul & body.

God bless you & Kathy & may he keep you both safe from all harm.

My most sincere & deepest love and a million kisses.

Your husband,
Bill

PS I love you xxxxxxxxxx for my to wonderful girl. I hope to be in your arms

PSS I adore you xxxxxxxxxx very soon kitten. L. Bill Xxxxxxxxxx

July 10, 1945
Koblenz, Germany

My Dearest Darling Janet and Kathy,

I received your July 2 letter to-night. I also received a letter from Jane. I got 6 Enterprises the A.C. & F book "wheels" and the Vets mag.

Boy oh boy I really had you scared didn't I? I am the boss of that family of ours—

OK darling you win, I except your case as good enough. I understand now why you don't have a maid. I don't think Nina is taking enough money. Ten dollars a month is only about $2.50 a week. I think she should get more, don't you? Tell her I said so. Please darling take it easy, don't work, take your time at everything. You must think of Kathy and I.

I hope to God you never have to have an operation. I hope your trouble clears up and that every thing will be OK.

Now that I am coming home you'd better be well!! God bless you.

Janet I know just what you are up against with my family, I know they have hurt you and made it very tough while I have been over here. Everything they have done is in the back of my mind and I'll never forget it. Now when I get home you and I will talk over all this and see just what can be done. That is all I'll say now—till later!

Oh so the puppies are "dogs" now, boy what fun I'll have "playing" with them. I can hardly wait!!!

Janet E. where did you ever get that joke? That's the best one I've heard in a long time. That one wins the cement bicycle!

Well Jan I got a good conduct ribbon so I have all two ribbons now. Today I saw one of the boys with all 5 battle stars on his E.T.O ribbon and it looks swell. I want all 5 of mine on. It looks so much better then that one big star.

When I get home you can cry all you want too I'll probably do a little my self. In fact I am quite sure I will.

To-day in the S&S it said the 35th would sail in Sept but I am very sure we will beat that by many weeks. I heard that we will be on the high seas in 3 weeks. I sure hope so. It was over the radio to day that the 35th was going home.

This evening we got our Cannon book and Janet it is wonderful, I am so very proud of it and I know every one that gets one will be also. Tell Nina I have one for her. I won't be able to send it till we get to Rheims.

We are leaving here early Thurs morning we have a 320 mi move. I don't know if we are going straight to Rheims or not but it looks very much like it.

Jan I may not be able to write for a few days but don't worry I'll be OK. Just so you know that I am starting my first leg of the trip back into your arms.

I should start and pack my duffle bag to-night I'll see how much time I have left. Janet I am afraid I'll have to get rid of all you letters, I'll need all the space I can get in that bag I hate to do it but it is necessary. I know you understand.

This is'not going to be a very long letter to-night_to tell you the truth I am so dam excited I can hardly sit still. Everyone of us are. Even if we don't leave for a month I'll be like this. Oh boy what a feeling.

I am going to address the books (envelopes) to-night. Then I think I read my Enterprises and maybe go to bed. I'll have quite a bit of work to do in the supply room to-morrow. We must load some of the things.

July 10, 1945

Well darling I guess this is all I have for my Report from Germany to-day. My dearest darling I do love and adore you with all my heart, soul and body. God bless you and Kathy and may he keep you both safe from all harm. My most sincere and deepest love and a million kisses.

Your Husband
Bill

PS
I love you
PSS
I adore you
XXXXXXXXXXX
XXXXXXXXXXX for my girls whom I shall see!

July 11, 1945
Koblenz, Germany
12:30 P.M.

My Dearest Darling Janet and Kathy

Jan dear this letter will be short—reason, I'll be very busy all day packing and getting things in shape for our move to Rheims to-morrow.

We are to leave early in the morning, 6:00 o'clock I believe.

Rumors from Regt. Have it that our boat docks to-morrow and if they don't slow us up at Rheims we will be on our way in two weeks. Don't count on it is only a rumor. We also hear our boat is the "Queen Mary", I hope so.

I am taking time out now to write, I want this letter to go out now.

As soon as I get a chance I'll write again, It may be a day or so but don't worry. You may not hear from me every day now but I'll do my best. If I get any mail from you to-night I'll have to ans it later.

I have some pictures I'll send, I found them in a German town back in Feb. I forgot I had them. They are pictures of the barracks we were in in Metz that was when the Nazi were in their power.

I am also sending you two sticks of gum one for you

and one for Nina.

Last night they said we could send out Cn. Books so yours in on its way.

Darling I am sorry but I'll need some money can you send me $25.00 fast. I don't have any at all. I borrowed $5.00 from Paul Thompson. I want some money when I get home. I hope it does'nt miss me, it may, give it a try anyway.

I can't believe that I am on my way into your arms. What a reunion that will be, I can hardly waite.

Darling much as I hate to I must stop now. We are loading the trailer with the supplys and I must go.

This is all I have for my last letter from Germany.

My darling I do love and adore you will all my heart, soul & body.

God bless you & Kathy & may he keep you both safe from all harm.

My most sincere & deepest love & a million kisses.

Your Husband
Bill

    P.S.
    I love you
    PSS
    I adore you
    PSS Those picures I discovered are in the bottom of

my duffle bag. I'll bring them home instead of sending them. Love Bill

xxxxxxxxx

xxxxxxxxxx for my girls.

July 16, 1945
Camp Norfolk, France
8:37 PM

My Dearest Darling Janet and Kathy,

I did not receive any mail from you to-day, I hope I get some to-morrow.

Well we have L&M, Regt Hq, Cannon, Anti-Tank and Sv Co's to process then we will be finished. I don't know if I will get some kind of a job again or not, I mean at Regt, if I don't I'll go back to suppy.

We were told to day when we go to the staging area we wouldn't be there longer then 36 hrs and we would not be at the port more than 24 hrs. Sixty hrs after I hit the states, I'll be home on a furlough-duffle bag and all. I go to either Ft Dix or Indiantown Gap-there is where I get the furlough, after furlough back to base camp-where ever that is. Usually the 35th draws a hell hole, I don't think it will be any different now.

Janet dear I stopped that one class E allotment. You see if I kept it up, I'd be paying the Army at the pay table. I'll loose my overseas pay and that is what I had the allotment on. You don't care do you?

After working all day, I worked from 6 to 8 in the supply, if I do something like that for the supply Sgt. he treats me OK. He ask me if I'd help, so I told him I would.

I like to work for him anyway. I am never short anything I need, if he has anything extra.

We have been turning in a lot of our stuff, so my duffle bag won't be as heavy as it was coming over.

Well darling this is a very short letter, please forgive me dear but I know you understand-and anyway I'll soon be home and that will be better.

Jan dear this is all I have for my Report from France to-day.

My dearest Janet I do love and adore you with all my heart, soul and body.

God bless you and Kathy and may He keep you both safe from all harm.

My most sincere and deepest love and a million kisses.

Your Husband,
Bill

PS I love you
PSS I adore you
XXXXXXXXX
XXXXXXXXX for my wonderful girls

Sept 1, 1945

Tidworth, England
1:37 PM

My Darling Wife

Well darling we leave here Tues to board the "Queen Mary", I understand we are to sail late Wed. night. Oh darling how anxious I am to get home to you. It will be like heaven to be back home.

I see now no man over 60 points will go overseas, so I guess I am safe I do believe if everything works out like it should, I may be out of the Army before very long. If they count up the points like they say they will I'll have 78 and believe discharge score is 72 or 75 I forget which.

I went to London on tues and had a wonderful time. I saw so many interesting things like the Tower of London, the Kings Palace, Westminster Abey (was in side) and all the famous places that I could possible visit in the short time I was in London. I'll tell you all about it when I get home It took us two hr by train to get to London. We left 7:30 AM tues morning and arrived at 9:30 AM. We left Wed afternoon at 3:40 and arrived in Tidworth at 6:05. I would have gone again yesterday if I had the money. I've seen quite a few large European cities, Paris and London I wanted to see most of all. Paris is prettier than London but I liked London better.

Darling I am ashamed of one thing. I wanted to send Kathy a cablegram on her birthday but I did not have the money. I'll make it up to her when I get home.

I don't know if you will get this letter before I arrive in the states or not. I would'nt doubt that it might go on the same boat. Sometimes they send air mail by ship.

My darling Janet I love you so very very much. This next week or so will seem so very long. We should arrive in N.Y. Sun or Mon. of next week. I'll call you as soon as I can darling.

I've been dreaming of you so much these past night, I have you on my mind night and day.

I am writing this letter at the Red Cross this gloomy Sat afternoon. After I finish I am going to read for the rest of the afternoon.

I have some kind of a detail to-morrow. I am not sure if it is K.P. or prisoner chaser. P.C. is the best job all you do is take the German's to the kitchen at 6:00 A.M. and leave them there, that is all you do all day. A man at 2:30 get them back and brings on the night shift. I like that job. I had it once before.

This is'nt going to be a very long letter because I'll have plenty to talk about when I get you in my arms. I know you understand.

Well my darling sweetheart I guess I'll leave you now, I hope now that the next time you hear from me will be by telephone,

My dearest Janet I do love and adore you with all my heart, soul and body.

God bless you and Kathy and may He keep you both from all harm.

My most sincere and deepest love and a million kisses.

Your Husband
Bill

PS
I love you
So very very much
PSS
I adore you
xxxxxxxxxx
xxxxxxxxxx
xxxxxxxxxx for my darling girls

Part Two

—

PHOTOGRAPHS

from the collection of Bill Golder

*Photo from Paris, France. My grandfather is in the second
row, third from the right. He is wearing his hat
and Eisenhower jacket.*

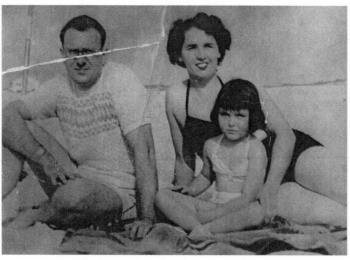

*The Golder family: Bill, Janet, and Kathy. Photo taken at Beach
Haven in 1949.*

Marvin William Golder, "Bill", 35th Inf. Div., 320th Reg., Cannon Company, in a foxhole near Gremecey Forest, France, 1944

Sgt. John Walsh (right). The other man is unidentified. Taken in 1944 or 1945.

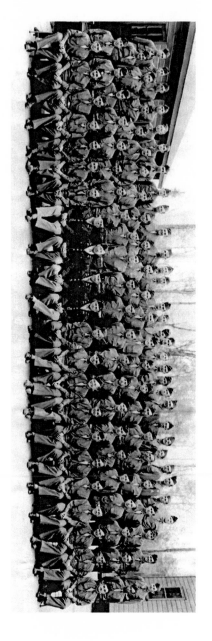

Cannon Company, 320th Infantry Regiment
Camp Butner, North Carolina, May 1944

128

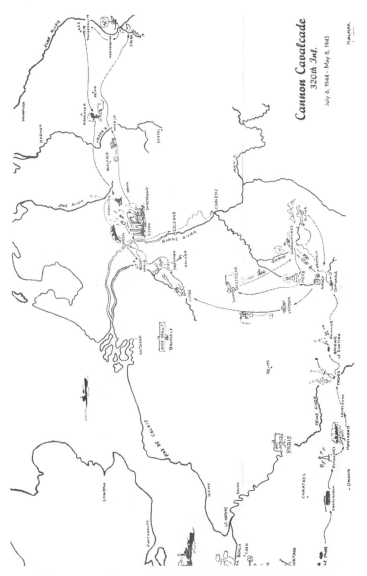

Map from the Cannon Company book, published in 1945.
Drawn by William Kalmar.

129

Railroad yards at Munster, Germany

Relaxing around the foxhole

*Bill Golder at the World War II memorial
in Washington, DC, October 2004*

131

Cannon Company in the field

Janet, Kathy, and Harry Mitchell

Part Three

—

CANNON COMPANY

the 35th Infantry Division Cannon Company
through the eyes of Sgt John Walsh

Thank you to Mr. Walsh for sharing his memories of the war. His willingness to share his experiences, made it possible for me to preserve the history of Cannon Company. His stories are a gift to be treasured.

Note to the Reader

—

Iconnected with John Walsh about a year after my grandfather passed away; although to me he is known as Mr. Walsh. John served with my grandfather during the war; in the 35th Division, 320th Regiment, Cannon Company.

Over the past 4 years John has graciously shared with me the history of Cannon Company; and his memories of that time period.

John was born in 1921. In 1939, he graduated Xavier High School in New York. He then went on to attend Niagara College and earned a Bachelor of Arts degree in 1943. He enlisted in the United States Army ROTC his final year of college. He was called up for active duty after he graduated; he was twenty-one years old. He entered the United States Army as Corporal; although he would later be promoted and reach the rank of Technical Sergeant.

While serving in WWII John was awarded the Bronze Star Medal. Recently, he was awarded the French Legion of Honor for his service in the liberation of France.

He has been an active member of the 35th Division Association since the 1980s and he is a former Association President.

It is both an honor and a joy to be able to preserve his war history. His stories have been such a gift to me that I hope this book will be the same for him. He has helped me gain a greater understanding of my grandfather's company during the war.

As in my grandfather's letters, these are John's own words and his memories.

–*Beth Miglio*

Cannon Company

—

The men of the 35th Infantry Division, 320th Regiment, Cannon Company served in the European Theater of Operations during World War II. They earned five campaign stars for their part in; Normandy, Northern France, Rhineland, Ardennes and Central Europe. This outline was put together with the collaboration of my grandfather's war letters, photos and the memories shared by Veteran John Walsh. In addition, the family of Veteran Walter Hoffman provided me information about his experiences he shared prior to his passing.

October 1943 – March 1944

Veteran John Walsh explains how Cannon Company was formed and how the men were prepared for war:

"The 35th transitioned from the West Coast, Camp San Luis Obispo, in the late Spring of 1943. After training at Camp Rucker in Alabama, we went on Tennessee maneuvers in late October or early November 1943 and finished in January 1944. Everyone got a 30 day pre-embarkation leave and we reassembled in Camp Butner, NC in February and March 1944. I was in the first group to get leave and was home by the end of January. About a third of the men were in each group. I got back to the 320th around the end of February.

During this period of time, there was a constant shuffling of personnel in and out of the division. Many were disqualified for overseas assignment for health reasons and others went to other outfits. In Cannon Company alone we must had at least 25 or 30 replacements after I arrived in late October. Because of the technical nature of our principal weapon, we needed people who could read and understand numbers. I do recall that a number of our replacements were bright men who had been slated to go into college training programs but were shunted to the infantry because of the manpower needs." (Information provided by John Walsh in an email 9/28/2010.)

On training for the war:

"While at Camp Butner we went into a period of intensive training to prepare for overseas movement. Each unit had to have a full complement, according to the Table of Organization and Equipment. All men had to pass physicals and qualify on their assigned individual weapons, as well as on the appropriate crew-served weapons. Our supply sergeant had been reduced in rank and I served in this capacity, until we got to Normandy. I had been promoted as Reconnaissance Sergeant but the company commander thought I would be more valuable in supply. In

Normandy I got my old job back." (Information provided by John Walsh in an email 9/30/2010.)

May 1944

The 320th Regiment, including the men of Cannon Company, completed their state-side training at Camp Butner. The men received orders and were relocated to Camp Kilmer, New Jersey. Camp Kilmer was the processing location for preparing troops for overseas shipment. The men received final supplies and medical attention before shipping off to join the European Theater of Operations.

On May 11th, the men boarded the SS Edmund B. Alexander. The next morning the ship sailed out of the Port of New York. It was a 14 day voyage to Liverpool, England. The trip overseas was crowded and left some of the men sea sick. The troops passed the time by writing letters to loved ones back home and playing card games. The letters written on the ship were transported back home after they reached England.

June 1944

Once the troops arrived in England they were dispersed to different locations. The men of Cannon Company were stationed at Okehampton, England. This time was used for final training and classes to prepare them for combat. The men were given occasional passes to visit the nearby towns.

June 6, 1944
D-Day: The Invasion of Normandy

John Walsh recalls his memories of that day:

"In our case most of us in our company had diarrhea as the result of a careless KP who left a bar of soap in a coffee urn. The only ones not affected were the non-coffee drinkers. I was awakened about 2 or 3 AM and had a difficult time finding an unoccupied toilet. By dawn most of us were so weak that we had to cancel most training exercises for the day.

We were kept busy in England training to make an amphibious landing. The grand strategy was to keep the Germans off balance and thinking that the Normandy landings were only a feint and that the real effort would take place at the Pas de Calais." (Information provided by John Walsh in an email June 6, 2010.)

July 4 – July 7, 1944

The men of Cannon Company crossed the English Channel on board a Liberty Ship; and headed for the Normandy Coast. They landed on the shores of Omaha

Beach near Isigny. They had entered the war in Europe.

John Walsh shares his memories:

"We kept training until early July and then went ashore at Omaha Beach without getting our feet wet. I was in a school learning how to combat load transports at the end of June. We had spent two intensive weeks on the subject and had spent the last days in solving a problem. Each team was scheduled to give its solution after lunch. While we were eating, an officer came in to the mess and announced that school was over and that we were to return to our units and leave for France the following day. As a result, we never learned whether we had passed or failed." (Information provided by John Walsh in an email June 6, 2010.)

July 9 – July 11, 1944
St Lo – Front

A few days after landing on the Normandy coast, the company carried out their first combat mission. On the evening of July 9th the men received their orders to move to the front lines outside the city of St Lo. The 29th Division was already engaged in the attack to liberate the city from the Germans. The men of Cannon Company established their combat positions and the next morning fired their first shot in the war.[1]

Cannon Company lost one of their own men in the early days of this fight: Lt. William Fessenden. He was a well-respected man and a Lieutenant. He was from Long Beach, California.[2]

The liberation of St Lo came on July 18th. The city was destroyed and lay in ruins as a result from the intense bombings.

Bill Golder wrote about his experience at St Lo; in his May 6, 1945 letter to his wife:

"As you know we hit combat July 9th, we went into position at dusk and 800 yrds from the enemy. I still was'nt frightened, I did'nt even give it much thought. I don't know why but I just knew I'd be alright.

The next morning we fired our first round into German positions, when I get home I'll tell you what I wrote on that first shell, a bit rough talk so I'd better not write it.

Things went along OK for a few days we still weren't combat wise-yet. My fox hole was so flimsy that a BB shot could have went through it. A day or so later we moved our guns about 50 yds from our first positions, we have dug the gun in and was sitting around talking when "Bam" a shell hit back about 50 yds from us and about 5ft from the truck. I hit the ground and waited but no more came in, we went and looked at the truck, it had more holes than a sieve. I forgot to say I had just left the

Making coffee

The 105mm cannon that was used by Cannon Company

Above:
Lt. William C.
Fessenden

Right & Below:
Observation and
reloading

truck about 3 min before. You can see why I say the Good Lord has been watching over me.

Four days after that shell came in we moved into an anti-tank position 200 yrds below our last position. We had our gun in a sunkin road. The banks on each side of the road were about 12 ft high and the road was so narrow a truck could hardly get through. We stood guard on top of the hill, 25 yrds from the bank. This one day Stubbs, Mask and I were on the hill and we decided to see what was on the other side of some buildings there so we started, we hadn't gone far till Stubbs hit me and knocked me down—good thing because an 88mm shell landed on the other side of the barn. I judge we were about 30 ft from it, but a barn between us. Two landed close by after we thought is was safe we ran behind some more buildings we had'nt any more than got there when 3 came in, the shrapnel fell all around us. That was the last near shell that came in there while we were in that position.

All through that position snipers would take pop-shots at us. One German, I think was bound to get me. I went after some wood to build up my fox hole, the wood pile was behind a wagon shed and I had to pass over about 25 ft of open ground, the hedge row stopped to leave an opening into the orchard then there was a gate and from the gate ran a fence to this building. To-continue, I gathered a few logs and started back when "zing" a bullet kicked up the dust in front of me, back I went to the shed,

I tried four times to get across that open space but each time he took a shot at me. So I waited—finally Sgt Johns came out and no one took a shot at him so I gathered my wood up and he and I took off to the guns.

All of this happened the first week of combat at St. Lo."

John Walsh shares his memories of St Lo:

"Our baptism of fire came shortly after we got on the line. Lieutenant Fessenden was killed while manning an observation post and attempting to direct our fire." (Information provided by John Walsh in an email May 11, 2009.)

John Walsh recalls meeting Lt. Fessenden.

"I was originally assigned to Company F but they were out in the field and it was suggested that I take a stroll around the regimental and familiarize myself with it. In the course of my walk I met Bill Fessenden and we had a chat, following which he told me that he wanted me in his company. He arranged a transfer and I only spent one day in Company F. Later Lt. Fessenden promoted me and used me in a variety of roles. In Normandy I was on an errand to scrounge up some telephone wire and when I returned got the news that he had been killed." (Information provided by John Walsh in an email July 24, 2010.)

Sighting the cannon

The gun crew

John Walsh explains the 105mm Cannon (Howitzer), and the responsibilities of Cannon Company with the 320th Regiment:

"Cannon Company had about 130 men and officers. We had 3 platoons and a company headquarters. Each platoon had two howitzers or cannons."

"Each cannon was manned by a crew of six. The crew was made up of two men who did the aiming. One man operated the mechanism that moved the gun from side to side to side and the other up and down. The other men performed the functions of preparing the ammunition and loading it into the gun. One man was in charge and responsible for seeing that the trigger was pulled on command."

"Communication with each crew was by telephone from the next level of command. After getting into Normandy and from there on, we would line up the guns in a field in a row. Identification of targets was made by the forward observers who were generally with the rifle troops in the lead of the regiment. The forward observers called in the location of targets by map coordinates to a company fire direction center, where calculations were made as to how and how many guns would be brought to bear on the target. Generally, one or two rounds of ammunition would be fired to check things out and then additional rounds would be fired to accomplish the mission."

"Communication was made by telephone or radio,

using radios that were carried by the forward observer's assistant. The executive officer or #2 was responsible for running the fire direction center with a crew of several men. The platoon sergeants and gun section sergeants ran the firing position. The gun crews never saw the targets, as all of our firing was done by lobbing the shells over the top of the forward troops. An important part of our operation was carried out by those responsible for bringing a constant supply of ammunition and distributing it to the gun sections which only had a limited amount on their trucks."

"Each gun section had a truck for the purpose of pulling the gun when distance was involved. Once the gun was close to where it would be set up it was manhandled by its crew into a firing position that had been designated by the sergeants and readied for firing. Practice drills had been carried out so that each member of the crew knew how to do the necessary jobs." (Information provided by John Walsh in an email August 22, 2008.)

Veteran John Walsh shares details of his job within Cannon Company:

"My principal role was to work with the company commander and executive officer to locate suitable sites for moving forward. We had to know at all times where our friendly troops were and that again was part of our command groups job. Communication was by telephone as much as possible, using a wire network that was prepared by higher headquarters. We also tied in to local artillery communication networks and were able to coordinate our fire with them. My crew and I stayed on the road most of the time and frequently slept and ate away from the company. The commanding officer wanted me to be aware of the developing situation and keep him advised of what was happening ahead of us. My crew and I had a jeep on which we carried all of our bedding and extra clothes, as well as a supply of food in the form of emergency rations." (Information provided by John Walsh in an email August 22, 2008.)

John Walsh on his friendships during the war:

"Ed Novey, Nick Belobaba and myself roamed all over France on recon together. We spent most of our time away from the company, reporting by radio or brief visits. We were the envy of many in the company for the freedom we had away from the routine of life at the gun positions."

"Nick was quite a guy. I thought he was going to get me killed trying to outrun a strafing German plane. I told him to stop so we could get into a ditch, but he was certain that he could do it his way and fortunately we hit a curve in the road and the plane missed us. He was a bit on the stubborn side, but a good driver and also a gutsy one." (Information provided by John Walsh in an

Left: Sgt. John Walsh (L) and Paul Gavzy (R)
Right: Walter Hoffman (photo submitted by Barbara Strang)

Foxholes in France. Names and location unknown.

email August 20 and 22, 2010.)

John Walsh shares his memories of Walter Hoffman, he knew him as Walter or Hoffie:

"Walter was a special friend in many respects. We were together outside St. Lo when we had a mine explosion that killed one of our men and put Walter in the hospital with a concussion. Later we were on our way into the 320th CP in Bioncourt when we were caught in a heavy artillery barrage and Walter was wounded and evacuated for hospitalization." (Information provided by John Walsh in a email dated July 28, 2009.)

Staff Sergeant Walter Hoffman II joined the company overseas as a replacement. He was awarded the Bronze Service Medal and the Purple Heart medal with two Oak Leaf Clusters.

Walter's memories of the war were documented in a book by Ellen Brennan Williams called *We're in This Together: 40 World War II Memories*. These stories from the book were told by Walter's children Barbara Strang and Paul Hoffman.

"He was a SSgt Communications Chief and his job was that of a scout; i.e. to go ahead of the troops as a look out and communicate the Germans' location back to the troops. He said it was important to find the highest points in the villages for the best results. The communications crew also had to lay and bury the lines, which sometimes

156

the Germans found and cut, so the Americans decided to lay a series of bogus lines, which bought them some time in heavy battle conditions. He spent a good portion of his time in St. Lo, France."

"He was driving behind enemy lines with a buddy to check equipment they had set up earlier, when nature called. They stopped next to a tall hedgerow; Dad got out first, heard a blast and when he looked back his buddy and the jeep were gone. Dad wound up on the other side of the hedgerow, and was soon picked up by those who were following."

"Another time he was in a foxhole, covered with wood planks, when German tanks started rolling right over his head. He thought he was a goner."

"During the Battle of the Bulge, Dad's unit was supporting a tank unit. The Germans, despite having better tanks, were outnumbered and low on ammunition. They started to withdraw and the infantry was sent to pursue them. The German battalion commander told his unit to start spreading out and dropping back their flanks. At a signal, the Germans would start firing directly on the infantry left and right. Dad was told by a scout what the Germans were up to and how close they were to hemming them in. They stopped long enough for our tanks to catch up. Shortly afterward the German commander ordered his men to surrender. Dad actually met the surrendering Colonel since he was near the lead United States tank.

The colonel heard Dad's name was "Hoffman" and probably figured his chances for good treatment were better with him and his men. He gave Dad his Deinstglas field binoculars and his personal sidearm, a Luger, which had been given to him by a German Field Marshall (crest and all). Dad hid the gun in a carton of cigarettes, crossed the ocean home and shortly after threw it away. He said it made him sick having it."

August 9, 1944
Mortain, France

In the weeks following the liberation of St. Lo, the men of Cannon Company were on the move again. The company received orders to take up a position outside Mortain, France. At Mortain, the Germans had completely surrounded a battalion from the 30th Division. The men were in desperate need of food and ammunition to push back the Germans. Reinforcements were dispatched to area to help free the battalion.

Cannon Company suffered another loss while aiding in the fight at Mortain. Lieutenant John Orr; from El Paso, Texas was killed in action.[3] Lieutenant Orr was an example of great bravery and was known to give encouragement to the men.[4]

The battalion was rescued on August 12th when men from the 320th Regiment reached the cut off unit.

Veteran John Walsh recalls his memories of Mortain:

"General Patton had nothing to do with us until after Mortain. In the early days we fought under the First Army and were on our way to join the Third Army when we were diverted to Mortain. The 3rd Battalion of the 320th was the first to reach the 30th Division battalion that had been surrounded. Colonel Northam had assumed temporary command of the battalion and was the leader in that effort. Cannon Company did a lot of shooting, mostly in conjunction with the 216th Field Artillery which had observers in aircraft. It was at Mortain that Lieutenant Orr was killed. Captain Smith had sent me to bring Orr back to the company area, since he couldn't see enough to do any good up front but he refused to come with me and ultimately was killed by machine gun fire from a German tank. I organized a detail to retrieve his body and take it to the morgue rather than to leave it for the Graves Registration Section."

"Mortain produced many heroes for the 320th. I can't name them all but it was there that Major Gillis did a great job with our First Battalion." (Information provided by John Walsh in an email dated May 11, 2008.)

Sgt. John Walsh was awarded the Bronze Star Medal for his heroic actions in the Battle of Mortain.

September 26 – October 31, 1944
Gremecey Forest, France

During this time period, the men of Cannon Company were in the region of Gremecey Forest. The drive across France was stalled due to lack of supplies. The company was ordered to hold their position and defend the forest. They endured heavy mortar and artillery fire to secure the area from the Germans.[5] The excessive rain fall received during this time made the mud an additional challenge for the men and the equipment.

Bill Golder wrote about his experience at Gremecey Forest, in his May 5, 1945 letter to his wife:

"I have one story to tell you that I never mentioned before because I never wanted to worry you. It happened Sept 30th that day we were shelled for about 4 hrs. Janet I never thought I'd live through that shelling the shells were so close that dirt covered us. Art and I were in are uncovered fox hole, we held hands and I said the Lord's Prayer. They threw everything at us from 88mm to 150mm. After the shelling stopped we pulled back to a new position. I was so nervous that I could'nt hold a match still to light a cigarette. We were lucky no one was killed but we had several injured.

From that day on I knew God was watching over me. He had to be for anyone to come out of that alive. That

Left: Bill Golder in one of his foxholes. He is eating pancakes from his mess kit. On his left side lies the insulated food container that was used to bring food to the soldiers in the field. Right: Lt. John Orr from El Paso, Texas.

Right: Nick Oprandy getting a haircut.

is an experience I'll never forget. It is in my mind as if it happened only yesterday. I said I'd never tell you about it till the end of the war, so now you know.

One shell hit our gun and our fox hole was about 10ft from the gun. One fellow had dug a fox hole just one shovel deep and when the barrage started he didn't think the hole was deep enough to get in so he went in with some other fellows-lucky he did because his hole got a direct hit. He was only 5 ft from our hole, so you can see how close they were too us. I think the nearest one was 3 ft.

We have had a few shelling since but never like that, thank God."

John Walsh recalls this period at Gremecey Forest:
"When we were at Gremecey, our company command post was in a house in the town of Bioncourt. We brought the men in from the field in small groups and gave them a chance to take a bath, shave and get a haircut. My radio operator, Ed Novey, had the idea of creating a bath house. The immersion heater consisted of a retort that was placed inside about a 40 gallon garbage can, filed with water. Each bather got a helmet full of hot water and two helmets full of cold. He stood in the tub and soaped up and had water poured over him to rinse him off. When he dried off, he was given a set of dry clothes that were swapped for the clothes he had been wearing. Periodically,

the dirty clothes were taken to a Quartermaster laundry for washing. There was no real ownership of the clothes.

In other instance we went to improvised bath and laundry operations, stripped and turned in our dirty clothes, bathed and were issued clean clothes.

Lt. Cammack was CO at the time and he, his driver and radio operator, my driver and radio operator and I stayed in town. At one point my award of the Bronze Star came through and we, along with Colonel Byrne, went out to the battery site and held the award ceremony there. I recall that it was drizzly overcast day and things were pretty muddy. This all was during late September and October while we were held up in our advance and awaiting gasoline and ammunition. Firing was restricted to a few rounds a day of harassing fire at intervals prescribed by higher headquarters." (Information provided by John Walsh in an email August 20, 2008.)

November 1944

By November the Cannon Company was situated in northeast Fresnes. Inclement weather threatened the morale of the men, forcing them to contend with constant rain, mud, and wet clothing. Many of them went for days without an opportunity to change into a dry uniform. As a result, trench foot was rampant among the ranks.

Captain Harvey Smith was awarded a promotion to

The men improvise laundry operations.
Left: Washing. Right: Shaving.

Cannon Company on the move

164

Driving through a town

A Sherman tank with improvised camouflage

major during this time. Cannon Company's new commanding officer, Captain Robert Ekstrum, was assigned to the unit after recovering from an injury sustained at St. Lo while leading 320th Regiment's Company B.[6]

On the morning of November 9th two men—names unknown—were killed by enemy artillery strikes.[7]

December 10, 1944

Cannon Company crossed the Saar River.[8]

December 12, 1944
Wiesviller, France

Cannon Company fired its first artillery round from France into Germany from this area near the border.[9]

December 1944 – January 1944
The Battle of the Bulge

The men of Cannon Company spent Christmas Day in Metz, France. The following day, December 26, 1944, they set out for Luxembourg; and entered the Battle of the Bulge. In mid December, the Germans had broke out and made a push through Ardennes region. This created a bulge in the line. The Allies were in critical need of reinforcements to stop the Germans from driving forward.

The company took up a defensive position; to assist in freeing several towns in Luxembourg. Boulaide and Baschleiden were liberated the end of December. After this, they continued the drive north and reached Bastogne on January 9th 1945.

By this time, the weather had become an additional enemy to the men fighting from their foxholes. There was no way to escape the below freezing temperatures and snow. It became an even greater challenge to withstand these conditions, since resupply of winter clothing was an issue. The lack of overshoes and gloves for the men were among the primary shortages.[10]

Some remembrances of the Battle of the Bulge Written by John Walsh 11/2/09:

We were on the Saare River when the Germans started to overrun our troops in the Ardennes. We had expected to advance into Germany through that sector. Instead we turned our positions over to the 87th Division and redeployed to Metz for the purpose of being resupplied and receiving replacement manpower.

We arrived at our assigned barracks in Metz before Christmas and were told that we would be there for a few days. Preparations for the holidays began. A visit to the Town Major (Military Governor) was undertaken and permission obtained to cut down a Christmas tree. Ornaments for the tree were made from paper and tin cans. Beer was obtained. Special rations, including turkey and the trimmings, were issued to each unit. Arrangements were made for all of our men to get baths and clean clothing. Nick Belobaba, my driver and our company barber, was kept busy cutting hair. Our kitchen crew went all out to serve hot food. Andy Greitzer, a skilled baker, made sweet rolls for breakfast as well as hotcakes with syrup.

Lieutenant Glenn Nowels managed to locate a USO troupe which put on a show for our company. Christmas was a delightful respite from the field. A number of our more talented members entertained with music. Ray Carroll did imitations of a German officer and one occasion answered the phone that way when Colonel Byrne, our regimental commander, called. All in all, we made the most of this brief vacation from the carnage that was raging around us.

On the morning after Christmas we set out for Luxembourg and joined the other troops engaged in liberating Bastogne which was being held by the 101st Airborne. The 101st had been deliberately moved into this key town and allowed to be surrounded by the German forces.

Our company set up its firing battery in a field near a farmhouse and its barn. The CP was in the house and our fire-direction-center in the barn. The weather was frigid but the gun sections all winterized their foxholes

One of Cannon Company's Saar River crossings

Left: Christmas Day in Metz.
Right: Lt. Lakness (L). He was severely wounded in the Battle
of the Bulge and did not return to Cannon Company.

and stayed inside except when firing.

My assignment was to roam around the regimental area and keep track of where our troops were deployed, exchanging information with battalion and regimental staffs. At night my team and I generally holed with the fire direction crew.

Lieutenants Cammack and Lakness were severely wounded by rocket fire, better known as "Screeming Mimis" because their whine made it impossible to judge where they were coming from and where they might land.

Everyone was tense because of the knowledge that specially trained Germans were posing as Americans. Because of a suspicion that passwords might have been compromised, sentries were challenging with questions that only real Americans would probably be able to answer. A favorite challenge would be to ask about Hollywood or major sports personalities. We limited our travel to daylight hours as much as possible.

I recall more than one occasion when our vehicles had problems on icy roads because of stops to answer challenges. We had sentries posted on a rise and frequently the challenged person had to slide back down to gain traction and start up again.

One of the duties of our company commander was to act as a special staff officer to the regimental commander and advise on the appropriate use of our weapons. Captain Ekstrum was not too well versed in the use of our cannons and most often assigned me to this job.

On December 31st I was ready to bed down for the night at about 10 PM when Captain Ekstrum decided that I should move to the regimental command post in case something dire occurred. I had about a five mile trip but it was a scary one. My driver and I were challenged at least a dozen times but never saw the sentry who had challenged us. When I got to the CP and reported to the duty officer, I was told to bed down for the night. In the morning I joined the other staff and liaison officers for a briefing and was told to stand by. One of the officers from a mortar battalion that was supporting us kept all of us entertained by doing imitations of Jerry Colonna, Bob Hope's sidekick. He was so convincing in his appearance and mannerisms that Colonel Byrne referred to him as Lieutenant Colonna, instead of by his real name which was Slater.

I also made trips to the 2nd and 3rd Battalion CPs and reported back to both regiment and to our own company. Both commanders were very friendly and appreciative of the fire support we were giving their troops. The 2nd Battalion Executive Officer was a particularly good friend, since he had been our company commander before being promoted.

When the road to Bastogne was opened, were rushed in and deployed to expand the perimeter. I went in a group with Captain Ginsburg, the regimental adjutant, for the purpose of being assigned an available building in which to establish our company CP. We were also allotted a location to set up our cannons. Captain Ekstrum was not happy with the building when I pointed out that we were only 100 to 200 yards from the known German lines. He left me and my crew in the building and camped out with the firing battery.

The 2nd Battalion CP was located in a building in the center of Bastogne and I was there on a visit when a rocket attack took place. Colonel Hannum, the battalion commander and I both dove for the same spot in seeking shelter. We banged heads and later we and the others had a good laugh over the fact that we were both wearing helmets and suffered no damage. If either of us had not been wearing a helmet, he would have ended up with a severe headache.

Our regiment continued the attack to expand the American sector and finally control was turned over to the First Army at which time we were sent to the Vosges Mountains because of a threat in that area.

In the course of retaking the area we saw the result of much carnage resulting from the German attack. We saw Sherman tanks with large holes in them and saw much destroyed equipment. One 105mm howitzer outfit we observed had fired their weapons at point-blank range against the enemy before sabotaging them.

The winter of 1944–1945

Ordinarily cannons are elevated and lob their projectiles. When timed fuses are used, the time of flight is calculated and the fuse is set to cause the projectile to explode when it reaches its target. In this case the barrel was parallel to the ground and fuses set to explode right out of the barrel.

In the intervening years since 1945 my wife and I have visited the Ardennes twice, once in 1954 and again in 1994. The countryside is beautiful and it hard to imagine the battles that were fought there in 1944 and 1945. The building in which our regimental CP was located is a small hotel and we had a delightful lunch there in '94. I was never able to identify any of the other buildings.

John Walsh
11/2/09

February 1945

Cannon Company spent this period in Germany, around Drenenen and Uettrath.[11]

March 1945

Cannon Company was assisting in the liberation of Venlo, Holland on March 2nd.[12]

April 16, 1945
Near the Elbe River

On April 16th, 1st Lieutenant Harold E. Ganzel's platoon was captured while defending an impromptu outpost situated in a barn near the Elbe River. Assaulted by German grenades, Panzerfausts, and even a flamethrower, the Americans were forced to surrender.

The German captors were then detected by Cannon Company's 2nd Lieutenant Kleber Trigg, who sighted them from an observation post half a kilometer away. He called for fire and the Company's six 105mm Howitzers obliged, scoring ten direct hits on the barn. Men exited the structure, hands raised, and it was assumed that the Germans wished to surrender. However, an interpreter sent to the barn reported that the men were American prisoners, and that the Germans had forced them outside to halt the Allied shelling.

After some time, the Germans attempted to escape with their prisoners, marching them across a field behind the barn. Trigg ordered precise fire and the artillery placed a volley of shells just above the Germans' heads. With explosions creeping nearer and nearer, the Germans retreated once more to the cover of the barn. Trapped and with few options remaining, they finally agreed to release the Americans. Thus twenty-three men from I Company owed their freedom to Cannon Company's deadly accuracy.[13]

April 30, 1945
Near the Elbe River

On this day Hitler and Ave Braun committed suicide. They were hiding out at Hitler's bunker in Berlin, Germany.

Cannon Company was in Germany, near the Elbe River. It is during this time period in April; that the unit got within 45 miles of Berlin. At the time they were attached to the 83rd Division; near Barby, Germany.[14]

From Bill Golder's May 4, 1945 letter to his wife:

"This morning we got wed Stars and Stripes with big headlines "Hitler Dead", that is really swell news. I expect any day now to see it come to an end. I'll sure be glad."

May 7, 1945
Victory in Europe (V-E Day)

Cannon Company is near the Elbe River when Germany Surrenders.

John Walsh was in a hospital in Paris, recovering from an illness. He did not return to the company until June.[15]

Bill Golder wrote a letter to his wife on this day. This is a few parts from that letter:

"Darling the War is Over! Boy what a day this is. Thank God I've came through this one OK. It goes in to

176

A sixty ton German Tiger tank

The Elbe River near Barby, where the 35th was
forty-two miles from Berlin

Cannon Company at Koblenz, July 1945

*The knocked-out bridge at Koblenz. Note the houses
on the near side of the Rhine.*

effect Tues at midnight but as far as that goes there is no more war. We have all day off—but being I'm on guard-guards always have been excused from all formations for 24 hrs. It is 9:00 AM here now and 3:00 in Berwick-boy I bet they are really raising hell at home now. I'd give anything to see that.

The war ended 11 mo to the day that we hit France.

I bet you are very happy you can't be any happier than your husband. Now I hope I'll soon be home-to stay. It still is hard to believe it is over, after all those months wishing and hoping and praying for it to be over and now it is. I hope all my praying to see you soon comes true. I have a feeling you will be seeing me before very long. I'll be so dam glad to get home it won't be funny. This is the first step toward our happiness, gosh darling it is so wonderful to have this war over.

I understand the states won't know about the war being over till Wed 12:01, in other words May 9 will be the real V-E day. Just 11 mo ago we went into combat.

It is a beautiful Spring day-a beautiful day for the war to be over which it is!

I just this minute saw a beautiful sight, 40 P47 flying in V formation went over us-Darling this is so wonderful I can't really believe it. Again I think I'll wake up and found out if is'nt true. How I wish I were with you now, we really would have a good time.

The Germans seem to be very well pleased that the

war is over. I think it is about time they are glad it is over.

I suppose now we won't have to have blackout curtains on the window, I hope they even turn on street lights-boy that will be something."

June 1945
Koblenz, Germany
Along the Rhine River

During this time period of occupation, many men were given passes and had a chance to visit cities in the area. When the men were not on guard duty they spent time writing letters back home, watching movies or playing cards.

Bill wrote several letters to his wife, while he was in Koblenz. This is part of his June 27, 1945 letter:

"Janet, I saw a crazy movie this after-noon it was Laurel and Hardy in "Bullfighters", I laughed till I hurt. There was also a sport picture, news reel and a short called "I won't play." It was a very enjoyable afternoon.

I went out to watch the 320th and 137 play ball but it started to rain so I came in, 320th was ahead when I left.

I believe I told you before the 320 baseball team is staying here with us, because they are using our ball field. I think the proper name for Cn. Co. barracks would be "Cannon Hotel" or "Hotel Cannon" we now are feeding about 200 men. Our little Co of 113 men sure has grown.

I am on guard to-night—third shift 10–12 at the jail. I stay there all the time till my last shift at 6:00 to-morrow eve. I sleep there also. It isn't bad, it is in side and we can write or read. I think I'll do both to-night. I don't leave till 10:00 so I'll get some writing done here before I go.

I hope I get some mail from you to-night, my darling.

Last night Raymond Carroll and I had the fellows just about crazy. For some reason or other the light on our room would not work and we wanted to read. We decided to read to each other, (his bed is across the room from mine) so we started to read "Sleep no More" a col-lection of horror stories. He read two and then I started another one. We started to read at 11:00 and quit just before 12:00—they did'nt say anything last night but this morning they raised Hell (in fun). We told them that if we had stopped in the middle of any of those stories—all three of them would have been mad. We have a good bunch here we get along fine, and we are always kidding one another."

July 1945

The war in the Pacific was still going on and additional troops would be needed. A point system was established to determine which men were eligible for discharge. The men with low points would be required to transfer onto the Pacific Theater war.

Cannon Company packed up and prepared to leave Koblenz, Germany. On July 12th, they relocated to Camp Norfolk. A camp was set up in a field near Sommesous, France to accommodate the troops.[16]

Bill Golder wrote a letter to his wife on July 11th. This is a few parts from that letter:

"Jan dear the letter will be short-reason, I'll be very busy all day packing and getting things in shape for our move to Rheims to-morrow. We are to leave early in the morning, 6:00 o'clock I believe. Rumors from Regt. have it that our boat docks to-morrow and if they don't slow us up at Rheims we will be on our way in two weeks. Don't count on it, it is only a rumor. We also hear our boat is the "Queen Mary", I hope so."

July 16, 1945
Camp Norfolk, France

Taken from Bill's July 16th letter to his wife:

"We were told to day when we go to the staging area we wouldn't be there longer than 36 hrs and we would not be at the port more than 24 hrs. Sixty hrs after I hit the states, I'll be home on a furlough-duffle bag and all.

I go to either Ft Dix or Indiantown Gap-there is where I get the furlough, after furlough back to base camp-where ever that is."

On July 18th, John Walsh was sent back to the States. He shares his memories of this time:

"I left the 320th on July 18th as part of the Advance Party for the division. We were scheduled for redeployment and eventual assignment to the Pacific. On arrival in the States we were given 30 days R&R, later extended to 45 days. I was sent to Kilmer for processing and reported back there. My recollection is that I got home around July 31st and reported back to Kilmer at the end of August and shipped to Camp Van Dorn, MS and then to Camp Breckenridge, KY. At Breckenridge all the rules changed. We were slated for inactivation and I ended up in Regimental headquarters in charge of supply. My task was to turn all the equipment and zero-out the books. The men returning to the division were either sent for separation or to another division, depending on how long they had been in service. After the 320th was inactivated, I agreed to stay around and moved to division headquarters. When the 35th was officially inactivated, I stayed with a unit of the 2nd Army and worked toward final cleanup. Most of the men came back on the Queen Mary toward the end of August." (Information provided by John Walsh in an email September 30, 2010.)

August 14, 1945
Victory in Japan, V-J Day – the end of the war

The next morning the men moved to Port of Le Havre for their transportation back to England. After they arrived, Cannon Company was stationed at Tidworth Barracks in South Hampton. It was the final stop before they were to board the ship for home.

During their stay at Tidworth they had the opportunity to visit and tour England. Several of the men went to London to visit the Kings Palace, Westminster Abby and the Tower of London.[17]

September, 1945
Coming Home to America

The day had finally arrived for the men of Cannon Company to board the Queen Mary. The ship set sail on September 5, 1945 and after the 5 day voyage they reached the shores of America. As they neared the coast, the sight of the Statue of Liberty stirred emotion in every man. They would soon have an opportunity to place their first phone calls to loved ones; who were anxiously waiting their return. After being processed at Camp Kilmer, New Jersey the men were granted furloughs of at least 30 days.

Bill Golder wrote one final letter before heading home to his wife. It was written at the Tidworth Barracks in England on September 1, 1945. Here is part of his letter:

"Well darling we leave here Tues to board the "Queen Mary", I understand we are to sail late Wed. night. Oh darling how anxious I am to get home to you. It will be like heaven to be back home.

I see now no man over 60 points will go overseas, so I guess I am safe I do believe if everything works out like it should, I may be out of the Army before very long. If they count up the points like they say they will I'll have 78 and believe discharge score is 72 or 75 I forget which.

My darling Janet I love you so very very much. This next week or so will seem so very long. We should arrive in N.Y Sun or Mon. of next week. I'll call you as soon as I can darling."

*Colonel Byrne awarding Bronze Stars to Lt. Nowels
and Lt. Schuster, with Captain Smith behind*

Writing a letter home

*Left: American,
British, and French
flags hang from the
windows*

Campaigns

—

A Battle Star was earned for each of these campaigns

Normandy
June 6, 1944 to July 24, 1944

Northern France
July 25, 1944 to September 14, 1944

Rhineland
Time limitations: September 15, 1944 to March 21, 1945
France, Belgium, Luxembourg and Germany east of the line

Ardennes
December 16, 1944 to January 25, 1945
Area forward of line: Euskirchen-Eupen (inclusive),—Liege (exclusive), east bank of Meuse River to its intersection with France-Belgium border, South and East along this border and the Sourthern border of Luxembourg.

Central Europe
March 22, 1945 to May 11, 1945
Area occupied by troops assigned to ETOUSA which

lies beyond line 10 miles West of Rhine River between Switzerland and Waal River until March 28, 1945, inclusive, and thereafter beyond East bank of Rhine.

The above information is courtesy of Cannon Company Cavalcade by James C. Murdoch.

Cannon Company mini-reunion in 1946. Seated around table: (from left) Bill Ellison, Walter Hoffman, Bernard Solomon, Tony Jannazzo, Tony Caterino, Joe Lopresti, Ed Novey, Nick Oprandy, Lester Grubman, Bayard Burlingame, Paul Gavzy, Bill Golder. Standing: John Walsh and Ray Carroll. At adjacent table: one of the men is Carl Rodamer but unable to identify the other man. Photo made at a mini-reunion of Cannon Company members from the New York area in November 1946 at the Fraternity House, 3rd Avenue and 17th Street, New York. Photo submitted by John Walsh.

After the War

—

Bill Golder after the war

Bill returned to his home in Berwick, Pennsylvania. He and his wife, Janet had two children. He enrolled at Penn State University. He earned a degree in vocational teaching; and became a teacher. He taught machine shop at Berwick High School from 1958 to 1968. He continued teaching machine shop at Columbia-Montour Vocational Technical School; until his retirement in 1981. After his retirement he became the curator for the Berwick Historical Society. Bill was extremely active until his death in 2006.

John Walsh after the war

John was commissioned in the Navy and left the New York area. He remained in the Navy until January 1949, where he served in the USS Ellyson (DMS19) and on the staff of Commander, Mine Force, U.S. Altantic Fleet. He met Geneva in 1947 and they were married that same year. They had four children. John and his wife settled in Connecticut; where they still live today. He worked as a management consultant until his retirement in the mid 80's. John has been an active member of the 35th Division

Association since his retirement. He has served on the Executive Board and is a former Association President.

Walter Hoffman after the war

Walter and his wife Lillian were married for 65 years and had eight children. He worked for the NYC Transit for one year. Walter then went to work for the FDNY for 28 years. After his retirement in 1975, he took up golf. Walter remained active and walked a 18 hole golf course 4 months before his death. He was 93 when he passed away in 2007.[18]

Bill and Janet Golder celebrating their
60th anniversary in 2001

John and Geneva Walsh in 1992. Submitted by John Walsh.

*Walter Hoffman and his wife Lillian. Submitted by
Barbara Strang.*

Dedication

—

In honor of the fallen men from Cannon Company

Marion L. Anderson
Paris, Texas

George Harris
Birmingham, Alabama

Wilber Dow
Pratt, Kansas

Claude Martin
Columbus, Georgia

Lt. William Fessenden
Long Beach, California

Walter Melton
Alton, Illinois

John Ford
Chicago, Illinois

Lt. John Orr
El Paso, Texas

"They shall grow not old, as we that are left grow old,
Age shall not worry them, nor the years condemn.
At the going down of the sun and in the morning
We will remember them."

From the poem "To The Fallen,"
by Laurence Binyon

Company Roster

—

Personnel roster courtesy of *Cannon Company Cavalcade* by James C. Murdoch:

* = Overseas Shipping List
† = Killed In Action

Adams, Archie T. * New York, New York
Ames, Harold Greenville, Texas
Anderson, Marion L. * † Paris, Texas
Anthony, Benjamin Juniper, Georgia
Bahret, Harold * Albany, New York
Bailey, Robert San Francisco, California
Baker, William Superior, Wisconsin
Baloga, Michal * Yonkers, New York
Barwick, William Coolidge, Georgia
Bassford, Joseph Hollywood , Maryland
Bednar, Mike * Detriot, Michigan
Belobaba, Nick * Kinney, Minnesota
Bibeau, Henry Worchester, Massachusetts
Bise, Archie Morgan, Texas
Bobo, Troy F. * Hope Arkansas
Boehm, Michael * Karlsrue, North Dakota
Borner, Phillip N. Freeport, Long Island, New York

Bowden, Ontee Little Rock Arkansas

Bowdoin, Jack * Columbus, Georgia

Bowling, Fred Arab, Alabama (transferred to 78th Division)

Bradley, Claude Cockran, Georgia (transferred to Regt Hq 320th)

Brady, William * Cincinnati, Ohio

Britt, Charlie Green Florida

Brown, Ellis Norman Park, Georgia (transferred to 78th Division)

Brungard, George Mill Hall, Pennsylvania (transferred to Co D, 320th)

Bruzda, Thaddeus * Cleveland, Ohio

Burke, William * Saginaw, Michigan

Burkhalter, David Athens, Georgia (transferred to Co E, 320th)

Burleson, Thomas, Hackleburg, Alabama (transferred to Co H, 320th)

Burlingame, Bayard * Cranstan, Rhode Island

Burton, Lauren Swannanoa, North Carolina

Byers, Edward Ervin, Tennessee

Byron, Wayne * Auburn, Nebraska

Cammack, Elbert * Lutz, Florida

Caraway, Hubert Columbus, Georgia (transferred to Reggt Hq Co., 320th)

Carroll, Raymond * Bronx, New York

Carter, Lawrence Pawhuska, Oklahoma

Catarino, Anthony Scranton, Pennsylvania

Caygill, Delbert Toledo, Ohio

Cahase, Frank * Big Timber, Montana

Chesher, Jack Davenport, Iowa

Chomack, Alexander Berlin, New Hampshire

Chrisicos, Nicolas J. Long Branch, New Jersey

Clark, Thomas * Fulda, Minnesota

Clem, Stanford Dallas, Texas

Coffeey, Marvin * muleshoe, Texas

Cole, Griffith Irvington, New Jersey

Cooke, Joseph J. Benson, North Carolina (transferred to XIII Corps, Camp Butner)

Cooper, Wade Ohleg, West Virginia

Cross, Jesse Mannington, West Virginia

Daymut, Mike * Sagamore, Pennsylvania

Deason, Bruce * Kansas City, Missouri

De Nourie, George * Orange, New Jersey

Dodson, Charles * Lubbock, Texas

Dorsey, William * Wichita, Kansas

Doty, Troy * Weeping Water, Nebraska

Dow, Wilber * † Pratt, Kansas (transferred Co H.,320th)

Dunham, Darrol * Nickerson, Kansas

Dutton, L. M. Hempton, Georgia (transferred to Regt Hq, 320th)

Ekstrum, Robert St. Louis Park, Minnesota

Ellison, William * Brooklyn, New York

English, Henry Chicago, Illinois

Estes, Jack Smithville, Tennessee

Evans, Richard * Roswell, New Mexico

Everett, Harold Duluth, Minnesota (transferred to Co F., 320th)

Evins, Paul * Syracuse, Kansas

Fallon, John * Trenton, New Jersey

Fein, Jack Newirk, New Jersey (transferred to Co G, 320th)

Feldman, Arthur * Bowling Green, Missouri

Feltem, Donald Kansas City, Kansas, (transferred to Co A, 320th)

Feltman, Vern * Dearborn, Michigan

Fessenden, William * † Long Beach, California

Finder, Henry Washington, Missouri (transferred to Co I, 320th)

Finley, Howell (transferred to Bt C., 216 FA Bn.)

Fleury, Clyde Lake Charles, La.....Blair, Nebraska

Ford, John * † Chicago, Illinois

Frey, Lenhart Lodi, California (transferred to Bt. C 216 FA Bn)

Furfaro, Vincent Scott Field, Illinois

Gargia, Jesus C. Solononville, Arizona

Gardenhire, Denver * Tulsa Oklahoma

Garlick, John Gilbert, Illinois

Gavzy, Paul * Rochester, New York

Geidl, Gilbert * Demiock, South Dakota

Golder, Marvin * Berwick, Pennsylvania

Good, Howard * Detroit, Michigan

Goode, Gene * Kansas City, Kansas

Gooding, James * Vista, Georgia

Greitzer, Andrew * Cambridge, Pennsylvania

Grant, Andrew Kansas City, Kansas (transferred to Bt C, 217 FA Bn)

Griffin, George Thomaston, Georgia (transferred to Regt Hq, 320th)

Grogan, James Norman Park, Georgia (transferred to Co. D, 320th)

Grubman, Lester New York, New York

Guzman, Pete * Bowie, Arizona

Hamsten, Clifton Cuba, Illinois

Hanlon, William Jersey City, New York (transferred to Hq 1st Bn, 320th)

Harrelson, Willie Mullins, South Carolina (transferred to Bt. C 127 FA BN)

Harris, George † Birmingham, Alabama (transferred to Regt Hq, 320th)

Heitz, Cecil Windor, California

Hewett, William Cheran, South Carolina (transferred to Regt Hq, 320th)

Hickey, Carl * Hiwassee, North Carlolina

Hiel, Anthony Akron, Ohia

Hinkle, James * Elizabethon, Tennessee

Hitch, Howard * Bremerton, Washington

Hodge, William Y Spencer, Tennessee

Hoffman, Walter Long Island, New York

Horn, Jesse Osawatamie, Kansas

Hook, James * Detroit, Michigan

Hosey, William Bessemer, Alabama (transferred to Bt. C 216 FA Bn)

Hudson, Herman * Georgetown, Delaware

Hunt, Julius * Mountain View, Oklahoma

Hyatt, Slyvester Henderson, Texas (transferred to XIII Corps, Camp Butner)

Jackson, Vernon Pineville, Kentucky

Jakubiec, Julian * Wyandotte, Michigan

James, Tilden * Benton, Arkansas

Jameson, David * Chicago, Illinois

Jandreau, Earl Syracuse, New York

Jannazzo, Tony * Brooklyn, New York

Johns, Derwood * Osawatamie Kansas

Jones, Cecil * Herington, Kansas

Jones, John Clanton, Alabama (transferred to Regt Hqs, 320th)

Jones, Royce * Akron, Ohio

Joubert, James Opelous, Louisiana

Kalmar, William * Goldsboro, North Carolina

Keene, Milton * Poland, Maine

Klug, Victor Corvallis, Oregon

Krieger, Irving Fort Meade, Maryland

Lackey, Richard * Norfork, Arkansas

La Croix, Robert * Detroit Michigan

Langbaum, Irving Bronx, New York (transferred to Hqs 1st Bn, 320th)

Langley, Albert * Prescott, Arkansas

Langley, Glen M. Pratt, Kansas

Lakness, Leslie * Los Angeles, California

Larson, Melvin * Badger, Minnesota

Layberger, Murray * Dryfork, West Virginia

Le Compte, Raymond * Detroit, Michigan

Levine, Robert * New York, New York

Lewix, Hunter Mesilla Park, New Mexico

Lietz, Arnold * Columbia, Missouri

Lightfoot, Cleo Tulsa, Oklahoma

Lindmier, Carl * Omaha, Nebraska

Linn, George * Zanesville, Ohio

Long, Harmon Dewitt, Arkansas (transferred to Bt. C, 127 FA bn)

Lopresti, Joe * Bridgeport, Connecticut

Lowe, Clinton Galex, Texas

Lynch, Paul * Indianapollis, Indiana

Maberry, Vernon Salt Lake City, Utah

McDougall, Raymond Brooklyn, New York

Marenda, Edward * Sundance, Wyoming

Martin, Claude * † Columbus, Georgia

Mask, Bernard * Fayettevile, Georgia

Matthews, Robert * Tacoma, Washington

May, Joe * Rosston, Arkansas

Mc Kelvey, Billie * Tulsa, Oklahoma

Melander, Russell Chicago, Illinois (transferred To 78th Inf Division)

Melton, Walter * † Alton, Illinois

Merriman, John Morgantown, Indiana

Mooney, Charles * Ellinwood, Kansas

Moran, Charles Houston, Texas

Murdoch, James * Galesburg, Illinois

Murphy, Harry Brookville, Indiana (transferred to Co D, 320th)

Nelson, Martin * Castle, Colorado

Newman, Walter Plymouth, Michigan

Nichilo, Frank Chicago, Illinois (transferred to Co G, 320th)

Norwood, Edward Richmond, Virginia

Nowels, Glenn Akron, Ohio

Novey, Edward * Bronx, New York

Oglesby, Francis Scott, Kansas (transferred to Co F, 320th)

Oprandy, Nicolas * Englewood, New Jersey

Orr, John * † El Paso, Texas

Owens, Frank * Johnson City, Tennessee

Patelzick, Ernest Newman, California (transferred to Bt. C, 127 FA)

Pearson, Harry Twinsfalls, Idaho (transferred to Co F, 320th)

Pekarek, Charles Flint, Michigan (transferred to Regt Hqs Co, 320th)

Peterson, Howard Winthrop Harbor, Illinois

Pinkley, Loyd Osawatomie, Kansas

Poage, Walter Ryan, Oklahoma

Points, Walter Gibson, Oklahoma (transferred to Bt C., 127 FA)

Post, Max Holton, Kansas (transferred to Co H., 320th)

Prislupske, John Johnson City, New York (transferred to Co F., 320th)

Puch, Ewaldus Freeport, Pennsylvania (transferred to Regt Hqs Co., 320th)

Quinn, Norman * Omaha, Nebraska

Rademacher, Franklin Bronx, New York

Rasmussen, Howard Chicago, Illinois

Robertson, Charles Lincoln, Nebraska (transferred to 1661 Sv. Ft. Custer)

Rodamer, Carl * White Plains, New York

Sado, Tulio Prest River, Idaho (transferred to Regt Hqs Co., 320th)

Saint, James Columbus, Georgia (transferred to Co M., 320th)

Sanders, Hubert * Bessemer, Alabama

Santillanes, Fernando * Chicago, Illinois

Schlobohm, Nolan W. Reading, Kansas

Schuster, Charles * Chicago, Illinois

Shettleroe, Wayne Hamtramck, Michigan (transferred to Co L., 320th)

Simpson, Winford * Boaz, Alabama

Smiley, George * Norlina, North Carolina

Smith, Harvey Denton, Texas

Smith, James * Crossville, Alabama

Snyder, Clyde Leavittsburg, Ohio (transferred to 2nd Bn Hqs Co., 320th)

Solomon, Edward * Brooklyn, New York

Songer, Glenn * Plainview, Kansas

Sorters, Barney Guntersville, Alabama (transferred to Bt., A. 216 FA)

Strandlof, Herbert * St Paul, Minnesota

Strimple, Robert Topeka, Kansas (transferred to XIII Corps, Camp Butner)

Stubbs, Arthur * Bowmansville, Pennsylvania

Studdad, J. C. Albertville, Alabama (transferred to Bt. A., 216 FA)

Stutz, William * Murdock, Illinois

Summers, James * Chattanooga, Tennessee

Surma, Louis Detroit, Michigan

Tanquary, Kent Kentland, Indiana (transferred to XIII Corps, Camp Butner)

Teffer, John * Spring City, Tennessee

Tenorio, Blas * Kyle, Texas

Terranova, Martin * new Orleans, Louisiana

Thompson, Clifford * Indianapolis, Indiana

Thompson, Paul * Jefferson City, Missouri

Trapani, Frank * Chicago, Illinois

Trigg, Kleber Bastrop, Texas

Trinkle, Vilas * La Cygne, Kansas

Urbaniak, Harold * Detroit, Michigan

Beteto, Richard Amity, Arkansas

Wahl, Ellsworth Los Angeles, California

Wailes, Augustus Carlsbad, New Mexico

Walsh, John * Brooklyn, New York

Walters, Alvin * Pickton, Texas

Weegman, Frederick * Minneapolis, Minnesota

Welch, Gordon Adel, Georgia (transferred to XIII Corps, Camp Butner)

Whitaker, Eugene * Big Flat, Arkansas

White, Charles Louisville, Kentucky

Wiley, Kenneth * Millboro, South Dakota

Winnicki (transferred to 216 FA)

Wood, James Washington, D. C.

Wood, Robert * Wichita, Kansas

Worth, Harvey (transferred to Bt A., 531 FA Camp Rucker)

Wright, Dexter Dunlap, Texas

Young, James * Ottawa, Kansas

Zarella, Dominic Waterbury, Connecticut

The following men joined Cannon Company after V-E Day:

Kekoni, Robert Chisholm, Minnesota

Radziwon, John Yukon, Pennsylvania

Ross, Louis Daniel Connellsville, Pennsylvania

Toney, Jerome Baltimore, Maryland
Trafford, R. B. Little Rock, Arkansas
Trevitz (no other information)
Schott, Curtis V. Atlanta, Georgia

Bibliography

—

320th Infantry, Public Relations Office. *Story of the 320th Infantry*. Hameln: Niemeyer, 1945. Print.

35th Infantry Division. *Presenting the 35th Infantry Division in World War II*. Atlanta: Albert Love Enterprises, 1946. Print.

Faubus, Orval. *In This Faraway Land*. Conway: River Road Press, 1971. Print.

Muller, Gusty. *Do You Know Luxembourg?*. Luxembourg: St. Pauls Printing House, 1945.

Murdoch, James C. *Cannon Company Cavalcade*. Neuwied: J. Strüders Publishing House, 1945. Print.

Williams, Ellen. *We're In This Together: 40 World War II Memories*. Reading: Aperture Press, 2012.

Personal documents, letters and emails.

End Notes

—

Certain specific facts presented in this text have been verified by the sources below:

1: Letter from Marvin Golder, May 6, 1945

2: *In This Faraway Land*, p. 166. Email from John Walsh, July 24, 2010.

3: Email from John Walsh, May 11, 2008.

4: *In This Faraway Land*, p. 229.

5: *Story of the 320th Infantry*, p. 27–28. Letter from Marvin Golder, May 5, 1945.

6: *In This Faraway Land*, p. 158, 382.

7: *In This Faraway Land*, p. 385.

8: *Cannon Company Cavalcade*, p. 123.

9: *Cannon Company Cavalcade*, p. 123.

10: Email from John Walsh, November 18, 2008.

11: *Cannon Company Cavalcade*, p. 124.

12: *Cannon Company Cavalcade*, p. 124.

13: *Story of the 320th Infantry*, p. 50–51.

14: Letter from Marvin Golder, May 24, 1945. Photo notes from Marvin Golder.

15: Email from John Walsh, July 30, 2010.

16: *In This Faraway Land*, p. 645.

17: Letter from Marvin Golder, September 1, 1945.

18: Information provided by Barbara Strang.